Towards Inclusive Education

Khalsa College of Education
G. T. Road, Amritsar

Khalsa College of Education, Amritsar, a premier institute of Teacher Education is a unique amalgamation of professional and academic excellence. The college started its onerous journey as a B.T. Department of main Khalsa College, Amritsar in the year 1954 and subsequently became an independent college in the year 1959.

The college is offering both Under Graduate & Post Graduate courses viz. M.Ed. 2 year, B.Ed. 2 year, 3 year Integrated B.Ed. M.Ed., 4 year Integrated B.A.B.Ed, 4 year Integrated B.Sc.B.Ed & PGDCA (TE).

Accredited 'A' grade by NAAC in 2003, 2011 and 2016, the objective of the college is to prepare passionate, innovative, secular teachers for 21st century with a focus to develop their competencies and chisel their skills required to compete in the world job market.

Under the able stewardship of the Management and the Principal, the highly qualified faculty of the college are making relentless efforts to provide training to the teacher trainees to become a part of the 'knowledge generating society' by enlarging their intellectual horizon.

With a determination to synthesize precept and practice, the college promises to build a social foundation for teaching skills which will enable the students to develop their potential to the utmost. A wide spectrum of programmes paired with flexibility, experiential learning and inter disciplinary orientation emancipate our students to explore their potentialities and hone their skills for fulfilling careers.

Towards Inclusive Education

With Special Reference to NEP 2020

Editors
Harpreet Kaur
Maninder Kaur
Deepika Kohli

SHIPRA

₹1250; US$ 50
ISBN: 978-93-91978-25-9

2023
First Hardback Published in India

Towards Inclusive Education:
With Special Reference to NEP 2020

Published by:
SHIPRA PUBLICATIONS
LG 18-19, Pankaj Central Market
I.P. Ext., Patparganj, Delhi 110092, India
Tel.: +91 11 2223 5152/6152; 96500 28065
E-mail: info@shiprapublication.com
www.shiprapublication.com

Message

Our journey as a nation began in 1947 and since then we have achieved a great deal in the 75 years but to get ahead further, we will have to resolve our chronic problems arising from our attitudes related to caste, religion and gender. With the growing complexity of civilization, this responsibility can only be managed and sustained with an inclusive and futuristic education system with a focus on personality development.

The initiative by Khalsa College of Education, G. T. Road, Amritsar to publish a book, 'Towards Inclusive Education' (with special reference to NEP 2020) is commendable as it would help the readers to understand the 'Constitutional values' and become sensitive to 'pluralism and diversity' as well as realize the significance of 'equality and fraternity' in real life situations.

I extend my warm wishes to the college fraternity for taking this great initiative.

May the Institution continue its journey on the road of excellence!

S. Satyajit Singh Majithia
President
Khalsa College Charitable Society
Amritsar

Message

The pressing challenges of equity, sustainability and inclusivity are further intensifying in 21st century. Appropriately, the National Education Policy (NEP 2020) has also envisioned higher education that is multidisciplinary, inclusive and equitable. India's education, especially its colleges and universities must rise to these challenges that address them through teaching and research.

The ambitious initiative by Khalsa College of Education, G. T. Road, Amritsar to publish a book 'Towards Inclusive Education' (with special reference to NEP 2020) is a great step towards compiling the innovative ideas/suggestions of the educationists and scholars from across the nation.

It will definitely help higher education institutions in bringing a comprehensive change in institutional outlook and remove barriers for achieving the goals of Education for all.

I convey my appreciation to this laudable initiative of Khalsa College of Education, G. T. Road, Amritsar.

S. Rajinder Mohan Singh Chhina
Honorary Secretary
Khalsa College Charitable Society
Amritsar

Foreword

Inclusive education, a phenomenon based on social justice, gives an equal opportunity to children with different abilities to get a quality education in the mainstream. The unique contribution that each student can make in society can be capitalized on only by giving them the equal opportunity for growth. Nowadays, inclusion has been a priority in the educational policies of almost every country including India. To achieve sustainable development goals and to ensure equity in education which is one of the important pillars of the Indian education system, inclusive education is one of the most important steps. The differentiation of inclusive education from special education and the rationale for identifying it as a need of the hour has been rightly explained in the book. The vision of becoming a global knowledge superpower is impossible without inclusive education as it is a way in which education is made accessible to all without any discrimination. This will also result in making education a fundamental right of every individual in the true sense.

This book has the potential to put forward the ways in which quality inclusive education can be provided to all in the current scenario. As the book has inputs from academicians and research scholars working in the education sector, it is likely to provide more realistic and practical perspectives. National Education Policy 2020 also aims at providing quality education to all and the productive suggestions from all the stakeholders will provide novel ways in which the suggestions of NEP 2020 can be put into actual practice. The editor has correctly identified the needs of the learning community and included fresh voices and perspectives in inclusive education with special reference to the National Education Policy 2020.

The inclusive education practices prevalent presently in the education system have been discussed in detail. The major strength of the book is the way in which it explained the ways of facing the challenges in providing inclusive education in mainstream schools. Researchers and academicians have put forth the key issues in the implementation of inclusive education and suggested the roadmap to inclusion based on their research findings. The critical review of the important provisions of NEP 2020 for quality and equitable education gives a realistic picture of the challenges that need to be faced to make inclusive education a reality. The challenges regarding the development of academic and social skills of not only children with different abilities but also of the teachers teaching them, need to be given consideration. Thus, not only the changes in the school education system have been discussed but the need for quality teachers for the implementation of inclusive policies has also been enumerated in the book. Teacher education for inclusion from both Indian and international perspectives has also been one of the key focus areas of the book. Above all, the commitment to the principle of inclusion and equity of all stakeholders is considered to be a prerequisite.

From my perspective, this book will be a great source of knowledge and a guideline for teachers working in inclusive educational settings. I appreciate the sincere efforts of everyone involved in the preparation of such a book which is so much relevant in the present educational scenario.

Dr. (Mrs) Deepa Sikand Kauts
Professor and Dean
Faculty of Education
Guru Nanak Dev University
Amritsar

Preface

India is built on hopes, aspirations and dreams of over 1.4 billion citizens. Providing avenues and opportunities through policy initiatives, planning and effective implementation can work as a catalyst in building a New India. This transformation is envisaged on the pillars of 'Atmanirbhar Bharat', 'Sabka Saath, Sabka Vikas, Sabka Vishwas', Digital India and Skill India among many others.

Indian youth is the key agent for socio-economic development and technological innovation. Their collective energies and vision is the engine of growth of our nation. Right type of education, skills and entrepreneurship opportunities to them can trigger overall socio-economic growth for our country. India is the youngest nation of the world; developing youth to unleash their full potential will only make India the global economic powerhouse.

The onus is on the educational institutions to handover the youth a country which they shall be proud of—a blend of modernity and tradition, infrastructure and services, growth and opportunities, development and sustainability, self-sufficient and imbibing world-view, intellectual and rational.

At the cornerstone of all decisions, the ray of hope has come through NEP 2020 which has conveyed the structural change in the educational system aiming to make India a global knowledge superpower as well as social justice and equality which is critical to achieve an inclusive and equitable society in which every citizen has the opportunity to dream, thrive and contribute to the nation.

Khalsa College of Education, G.T. Road, Amritsar invites the ideas and experiences of the research scholars, teachers, teacher educators, administrators and experts from across the nation on the inclusivity in different aspects of our education system and the futuristic vision of the recently released NEP 2020.

The views, perceptions and thoughts of experts have been compiled and presented in an edited book, *Towards Inclusive Education (with special reference to NEP 2020)*. The perceptions and thoughts given by the experts on various sub-themes clearly indicate that successful inclusive education happens primarily through accepting, understanding and attending to student differences and diversity, which can include the physical, cognitive, academic, social and emotional aspects. Teachers training programmes, adapted curriculum, teachers' attitudes, materials, equipment provision and financial resources are essential for the successful implementation of Inclusive Education.

Certain contributors remark that it should be obligatory for the Union and State governments to earmark funds and ensure opportunities for welfare and development through Gender Budgeting, Budgeting for Children, Scheduled

Caste Sub Plan (SCSP) and Tribal Sub Plan (TSP). It must be ensured that direct and quantifiable benefits are delivered to the target group, so that objective of Social Inclusion is achieved.

The private sector, public sector and civil society have to work in tandem in empowering youth. Inclusive growth and development are the keywords that will harness our demographic dividend.

Dr. Harpreet Kaur
Dr. Maninder Kaur
Dr. Deepika Kohli

Contents

1

Equity in National Education Policy 2020

Opportunities and Challenges

Harpreet Kaur (Dr.)*

Introduction

On July 29, 2020, when India was battling the first wave of the Covid pandemic, the National Education Policy 2020 (NEP 2020) was launched with an objective to re-imagine education in India. The incredible launch of NEP 2020 came 34 years after it was last revised in 1986. Before its launch NEP 2020 had undergone comprehensive consultative process with all the key stakeholders to create a visionary policy that could speak of the aspirations of young India. No doubt, the initiatives taken by agencies like NITI Aayog's School Education Quality Index (SEQI), the Sustainable Action for Transforming Human Capital in Education (SATH-E), and many district programmes gave further impetus to the systematic agenda. No doubt well timed and reformist, it marks a historic milestone in the country's education system.

The National Education Policy has opened a small window for the long-awaited reforms. The change in nomenclature from the outdated notion of Human Resource to a robust Ministry of Education ensures the small but definite new beginning. NEP calibrates with the system's need to focus holistically on the most critical tenets of Access, Equity, Infrastructure Governance and Learning.

National Education Policy 2020 starts with a wonderful preamble and vision. To quote the report, the vision of India's new education system as accordingly has been crafted to ensure that it not only touches the life of each and every citizen, consistent with his ability to contribute to many growing developmental imperatives of this country but also towards creating a just and equitable society. The NEP is based on 22 fundamental principles and it envisions an education system that is deeply rooted in India and will contribute towards the transformation of Bharat into an equitable and vibrant knowledge society, by providing quality education to all and thereby making India a sustainable global knowledge super power.

The pivotal role that a formalised system of Education plays for the development of a just, fair and knowledge society has been emphasized

* Principal (Offg.) Khalsa College of Education, G.T. Road, Amritsar

since ancient times because an appropriate education provided to the citizens influences the direction of their lives. For this Article 26 of the Universal Declaration of Human Rights (1948) emphasizes that Education systems worldwide should make significant strides to make education accessible to its citizens. This is possible only if educational opportunities are provided to all without any segregation and isolation of ethnic and linguistic minorities, those with disabilities and also those who face learning difficulties due to language barriers and are at the risk of Educational exclusion. The International Agenda being adopted by all countries for Education is focusing on Inclusive Education. The sustainable Goal (No. 4) states, "Ensure Inclusive and Equitable Quality Education and promote life long learning."

Inclusive Education: NEP 2020

Inclusive Education aims at providing quality education, rich and meaningful learning experiences to all so that we can advance towards more equitable societies and work upon the life chances of millions of marginalised and vulnerable people all over the world. Inclusive Education is not merely physical placement of students in mainstream classrooms but it is creating a society where students feel that their whole being matters and they too can be productive members of the society.

No doubt, National Education Policy 2020 lays emphasis on restructuring the whole system with the aim of ensuring the wide range of opportunities to all in curriculum, pedagogy and recreational activities. But there are certain facts of Exclusion that are very substantial. The road to achieve Inclusive Education is not smooth and is full of varied challenges and opportunities

Challenges before NEP

India's education landscape is not equal. The inequalities manifest themselves in the form of differences based on caste, class, gender and geographical location but NEP neglects the disquietude and ambitions of the young, especially first generation learners. Young people from the poor and disempowered background who are not only deprived of easy access but when it comes to studying in colleges they are dependent on external funding. Those at the bottom of the socio-economic ladder are more likely to be studying Humanities than a professional course. It is surprising that when the policy identifies the major problems faced by the Higher Education System in India (section 9.2), it makes no mention of the dismal of funds for the Higher Education Sector.

Due to this lack of public investment, almost 80 per cent of colleges are private and majority of public universities are in the process of being privatized or are shifting to self financing courses. Although, average tuition fee in central universities is nominal, the students cannot afford the add-on expenses. For example, in Allahabad University tuition fee is approximately Rs. 1,000 annually but the boarding costs Rs 45,000 to one lakh annually is detrimental for most poor students. The data indicates that almost six out of seven students enrolled in central universities fail to afford economical accommodation and the policy is silent on this issue.

If the government is committed to provide education to the socio-economic marginalized, then it is possible only through public funded education. Yet, when the policy emphasizes on improving Access to Education and says that there shall, by 2030, at least one large multi-disciplinary HEI (Higher Education Institution) in every district, but it does not mention that this HEI will be publically funded. The failure to highlight the funding issue as crucial problem with the education system and the absence of any timebound redressal policy, especially in the face of decreasing expenditure (from 4.14% in 2014 to 3.3% in 2020) is a surrender. Merely a statement of intent to increase funding is not sufficient.

Since, in the past three decades, India's socio-economic landscape and the educational field have undergone radical privatization. There are about fifty thousand institutions of higher learning in India and surprisingly out of them 70 per cent are private, and they cater to more than 35 million students. Although, in the past 20 years, Access, Equity and Quality have become a jargon, yet in the past three years approximately 2400 students have dropped out IITs, almost half of them belonged to Scheduled Tribes and Schedule Caste.

Thirteen years ago, caste discrimination and growing suicides among the Dalits Adivasis in elite institutions were pointed out by Thorat Committee report but the government just ignored it. According to MOS report — Hansraj Gangaram Ahis —26,500 students committed suicide between 2014-16 but no policy came in place to deal with these trends even after Rohit Vermula's suicide and sadly, even NEP is completely silent on these issues.

It is depressing that our education system has been producing youth who are self centered and have a inhumane parochial commitment to their caste but not to the society at large. It is disheartening that every year, about 600 manual scavengers die cleaning the sewers; but our policy makers, educationists and engineers from elite IIT's have miserably failed to think critically to end such an inhumane practice. The division created by caste is firmly stamped into our system. Many colleges as well as hostels are named after castes like Vaishya college, Jat school, Brahmin college, Rajput hostel, Reddy school etc. A child growing up hearing these names cannot be expected to act as active agent of the reproduction of caste!

Seventy-five per cent of the six million children currently out of school belong to socially marginalized communities (32.4% Dalits, 25% Muslims and 16.4% Tribals) as reported in Oxfam report.

We must not forget that the goal of education is to indoctrinate a human approach to understand the pain of fellow countrymen. Similarly, critical thinking is about recognizing social privileges and making sincere efforts for maintaining equality in society only then the "ethical, moral principles and values", so vehemently emphasized by NEP would be achieved.

Moreover, through the NEP, the government promises to bring in innovation, diversity, inclusion and a multi-disciplinary approach to inculcate critical thinking. In reality, the government has completely left out chapters on social movements, federalism, citizenship, nationalism and secularism from class +1 political science syllabus.

No doubt, NEP recommendation's for primary education to be conducted in the mother tongue is ambitious, but it will further add to the existing rural/small town-urban divide that is Hindi-Hinglish-English that has already caused great damage to the socially marginalized.

Like the previous policies the NEP's vision looks assuring but does not seem to bring about the structural changes needed for a more inclusive education system. It requires a well thought of perspective from the ground level to bridge the institutional and epistemic divide to create a balance between the humanitarian and utilitarian goals of education.

While looking at the moon, we should not ignore the manholes on the ground. Moreover, the quality of infrastructure in rural and urban areas cannot be compared. Except for Kerala, Punjab and Sikkim, the quality of infrastructure in rural areas is far inferior and that further contributes towards this divide.

Any policy such as the NEP is as good as its implementation. It also cannot be cast in stone. There has to be an inbuilt mechanism for a periodic review.

Recommendations

Policy initiatives for inclusion and equity that are specific or that need strengthening are as follows:

- Emphasis on policy actions for students from under represented groups
- Establishment of education zones
- Availability and capacity development of teachers
- Creation of inclusive environment
- Maintaining database of students
- Financial support to individual students
- Targeted funding and support for inclusion and access to districts and institutions
- Coordinated and integrated policy implementations to support underrepresented groups
- Emphasis on education of girls
- Partnerships with states and community organizations for girls education
- Fostering women's participation and leadership in education
- Prioritizing school safety and security
- Addressing social morals and gender stereotypes that encourage school non-attendance

- Gender sensitization in schools
- Education of children belonging to SC communities and tribal communities
- Translating learning material
- Education of children from urban poor families and transgender children
- Focussed efforts on Educational Access
- Emphasis on role of social workers and counsellors
- Education of children with special needs.

There is need to create a culture of change right at the school level. All participants in the school Education system including teachers, principals, administrators, social workers, counsellors and students need to be sensitized to the requirements of all students — the notions of inclusion and equity, the respect and dignity of all persons. Such a culture will be the best to help individuals to become empowered persons who in turn will enable society to transform into one that is responsible towards its most vulnerable citizens.

References

Govinda, R. (2016). Transforming Indian school education: Policy concerns and Priorities. *Yojana*, *60* (1), 7-10.

Govinda, R. (2020). NEP 2020: A critical examination. *Social Change*, *50* (4), 603-607.

Kumar, P., & Wiseman, A. W. (2021). Teacher quality discourse in India: A national reform agenda content analysis. *Teaching and Teacher Education*, *107*, 103504.

Government of India (2020). The National Education Policy, MHRD: New Delhi https://mhrd.gov.in/sites/upload_file:///E:/EducationBook/NEP_Final_English.pdf.

Planning Commission (2007). *The Eleventh Five Year Plan 2007-2012* Vol. I, II & III Government of India: New Delhi.

2

National Education Policy 2020
A Roadmap to Inclusive Education

Maninder Kaur (Dr.)*

Introduction

The National Education Policy 2020 (NEP 2020) is formulated in a new economic and socio-political context. This context is widely conditioned by the emergence of ICT-driven knowledge economy in India on the one hand, and stagnation of first mass of population in a state of limited access to quality education and skill development opportunities on the other. This context is again delineated by the growing demand for life-long learning, arousal of new occupational aspiration, and increasing physical mobility of population across the space and the resurgence of the forces of cultural nationalism and huge concentration of young population in the demographic landscape of the society. However, notwithstanding the increasing rate of literacy and education, their spread has been uneven among social groups in India owing to historical, social and geographical considerations. Social inequality and exclusion has remained embedded with the unequal expansion of the bases of knowledge and skill in the society in one way or the other. Such inequality and expansion is widely depicted in the arena of higher education in India. The NEP 2020 has remained grounded itself within these scenarios and has claimed to use education to be an effective tool to transform the course of the society towards the equitable and inclusive direction of a knowledge driven era. As against this backdrop the key question: What have been the commitments of the aspirations NEP 2020 in ascertaining equity and inclusion in higher education?

Vision of NEP 2020

The National Education Policy 2020 has envisioned education system firstly, to contribute directly to transforming India sustainably into an equitable and vibrant knowledge society, by providing high-quality education to all, and thereby making India a global knowledge superpower (NEP 2020:6) and secondly, to achieve social justice and equality, critical to achieving an inclusive and equitable society in which every citizen has the opportunity to dream, thrive, and contribute to the

*Associate Professor, Khalsa College of Education, Amritsar

nation. It proposes to create a new system that is aligned with the aspirational goals of 21st century education, including the aspiration of the Socio-Economically Disadvantaged Groups (SEDGs) (NEP 2020:3-4) like those of the SEDGs based on socio-cultural identities (such as Scheduled Castes, Scheduled Tribes, OBCs, and minorities), geographical identities (such as students from villages, small towns, and aspirational districts), disabilities (including learning disabilities), and socio-economic conditions (such as migrant communities, low income households, children in vulnerable situations, victims of or children of victims of trafficking, orphans including child beggars in urban areas, and the urban poor (NEP 2020: 24). It has also additionally recognised the special and critical role that women play in society and in shaping social mores; therefore, providing a quality education to girls is the best way to increase the education levels for these SEDGs, not just in the present but also in future generations (Ibid: 6).

Inclusive Education: Indian Context

Although post-Independence, India witnessed a lot of developments in the field of education none of them benefited the disabled children to a large extent. The main problem faced by the Special Education system was lack of teachers qualified to teach the children with special needs. In the past, there had been other programmes as well which were introduced to improve the educational quality like Operation Blackboard by the Ministry of Human Resource Development in 1987, the Lok Jumbish in 1992 and the District Primary Education Programme by the Ministry of Human Resource Development in 1993. These programmes were based on various ways of improving the overall infrastructure, the curriculum, human resource, and on ways to improve the achievement levels of the learner. The Ministry of Welfare in 1974 launched a scheme for Integrated Education for Disabled Children (IEDC). Under this scheme, educational opportunities were to be provided to children with disabilities in the normal schools so as to ensure they remain in the educational system and do not drop out. It provided for full financial assistance for the education of such children. In 1987, the Project for Integrated Education Development (PIED) was introduced to strengthen the IEDC scheme. This project was introduced with the assistance of UNICEF. It was carried out in a few blocks of ten selected States of India where all the schools of the blocks were converted into integrated schools. The teachers of these schools were given training to handle the needs of children with disability and an external evaluation of this project showed that due to the implementation of such integrated schools, the enrolment as well as retention of students with disability was higher; the awareness about education in general schools regarding those with a disability increased and also the teachers felt that they had become better teachers by teaching disabled children. However in 1982, the implementation of the IEDC was transferred to the Department of Education and in 1986 the education of these children was brought under the Equal Education Opportunity Provision under the National Policy on Education (NPE). Under this, the Programme of Action states that every child with disability who can be educated in general school should not be put in special school. In addition, those children who are studying in a special school should be integrated into general one after they acquire skills pertaining to daily living, communication and basic living. This Programme of Action not just emphasised on the principle of integration but made it an integral component of all the basic ongoing projects like the non-formal education, adult education, etc. There have been other schemes like the Integrated Education for Disabled Children and the Inclusion. Education of Children and Youth with Disabilities which provide for financial assistance to help include children with disabilities in the mainstream but along with that there has been an increase in the number of special schools as well. The policies on education have to recognise the role played by the other policies at the national level and has been acknowledged in other policies such as the National Policy on Early Childhood Care and Education (ECCE) put forth in 2013, the National Youth Policy (NYP) of 2014 and the national policy of Skill Development and Entrepreneurship 2015 in addition to various other policies of the state.

Equity and Inclusion in Higher Education

Since children with disabilities form a very significant number of out-of-school children, it becomes vital that·their needs are addressed by the schools and appropriate authorities. In light of this, the National Education Policy 2020 will ensure that students with varying levels of disability, which includes visual, loco motor, speech and hearing, and neurodevelopment disorders are given the opportunity to take part in the general educational process. The policy refers to these children as Children with Special Needs (CWSN). It also states that where the level of difficulty is great, there provisions for special schools will be made. Additionally, it lays special emphasis on the training and recruiting of teachers who will be able to teach in an inclusive classroom. It also recommends the setting up of boards which will oversee as well as guide the schools in addressing the needs of especially those children with a learning disability. This will be particularly beneficial as special programmes by the government for students with learning disabilities do not exist at the moment. India and UNCRPD "The UN Convention on the Rights of Persons with Disabilities" and its Optional Protocol (UNCRPD) was adopted on 13 December 2006 at the United Nations Headquarters in New York, and was opened for signature on 30 March 2007. The Convention stated that the government should promote the 'inclusion' of children in normal schools instead of their 'integration'. This means that the schools should be adapted in a way to adjust the child with disability rather than the child adjusting to the school curriculum. India needs to adopt strategies for inclusion and make amendments to its current laws. In addition to this, more funds need to be allotted for the education of children with disabilities. In fact, providing Inclusive Education is equal to or less than the cost incurred for providing education in a segregated school. This is so as the establishment of segregated school will incur the cost of infrastructure as well as the administration whereas in Inclusive Education, the infrastructure is already in place, just the way of teaching needs to be changed. A major concern in adopting the Inclusive Education in India is the training of teachers where the average size being about forty students to one teacher. In such situations it becomes difficult to provide individual attention to those students who need it. This also calls for training the teachers to work with students of different abilities. Many times, the teachers are not willing to admit students who are disabled in the classroom. In addition, in India, there is provision for either Special Education or mainstream and thus no teacher is prepared for both. The country lacked appropriate laws as well as the fiscal and human capacities to implement these laws. A major difficulty for the Indian educational system was to figure out as to how to bring Special Education to the poor, the lower castes, and the rural regions, when in fact even regular education is not accessible to these sections. Additionally, while there is a shortage of Special Education teachers, it is a challenge for the parents as well as the families who do not have proper access to these services. An attempt has been made to rectify the above mentioned lacunas in the form of the recently passed Rights of Persons with Disabilities Act, 2016. In this Act, there have been many new and welcome changes, in accordance to the UNCRPD. The National Education Policy 2020 states that in addition to the Rights of Children to Free and Compulsory Education Act, 2009, it will be the duty of the educational institutions to provide not just equal educational opportunities but also opportunities for sports and recreation. Additionally, the accessibility of the structures would be kept in mind, which would also include transport facilities. Not just the physical accessibility, but the NEP also lays down plans for suitable pedagogical adaptations to be made in the classrooms. Finally, it also talks about the employment of teachers who are trained and have a disability themselves. This simultaneously not just takes into concern the proper environment for education, but also ensures employment of PWDs in the field of teaching. National Education Policy 2020 envisions an India-centric education system that contributes directly to transforming our nation sustainably into an equitable and vibrant knowledge society by providing high-quality education to all. The policy also states that the Government of India shall constitute a 'Gender Inclusion Fund' to provide equitable and quality education to all girls and transgender students. The States shall use this fund to implement the Central Government's policies for assisting female and transgender students, such as provisions for toilets and sanitation, conditional cash transfers and bicycles. The fund will enable states to support 'community-based' interventions. The policy says that the Centre and states shall work together to increase public investment in education to 6% of the gross domestic product, from the current 4.43%.

Further as per the New Policy

- Barrier-free access to education will be enabled for all children with disabilities in the New Education Policy.

- Knowledge on how to teach children with specific disabilities will be an integral part of all teacher education programmes under the New Education Policy.
- Assistive devices and appropriate technology-based tools, language-appropriate teaching-learning materials will be made available.
- NIOS will develop high-quality modules to teach Indian Sign Language, and to teach other basic subjects using Indian Sign Language.
- Following the RPWD Act, 2016, children with benchmark disabilities shall have the choice of regular or special schooling. Resource centres in conjunction with special educators will support the rehabilitation and educational needs of learners with severe or multiple disabilities.
- Under the NEP schools and school complexes will be provided resources for the integration of children with disabilities, recruitment of special educators with cross-disability training, and for the establishment of resource centres.
- The fund (Gender Inclusion Fund) will be available to States to implement priorities determined by the Central Government critical for assisting female and transgender children in gaining access to education (such as the provisions of sanitation and toilets, bicycles, conditional cash transfers, etc.).
- Steps will be taken to ensure decent and pleasant service conditions at schools. Adequate and safe infrastructure, including working toilets, clean drinking water, clean and attractive spaces conducive to learning, electricity, computing devices, and Internet, library and sports and recreational resources will be important to provide to all schools in order to ensure that teachers and students including children of all genders and children with disabilities, receive a safe, nonviolent, inclusive and effective learning environment and are comfortable and inspired to teach and learn in their schools.
- To help ensure that schools have positive learning environments, the role expectations of principals and teachers will explicitly include developing a caring and inclusive culture at their schools, for more effective learning for all, and for the benefit of all in their communities.
- Teachers will be given more autonomy in choosing finer aspects of pedagogy, so that they may teach in the manner that they find most effective for the students in their classrooms and communities. Teachers will focus on socio-emotional learning, which is a critical factor in any student's holistic development.
- The policy also states that there is an urgent need for additional special educators for certain areas of school education. Some examples of such specialist requirements include subject teaching for children with disabilities/*divyang* children at the middle and secondary school level, including teaching for specific learning disabilities. Such teachers would require not only subject-teaching knowledge and understanding of subject-related aims of education, but also the relevant skills for and understanding of such special requirements of children. Therefore, such areas could be developed as secondary specialisations for subject teachers

or generalist teachers, during or after pre-service teacher preparation. They will be offered as certificate courses, in the pre-service as well as in-service mode, either full time or as part-time! blended courses — again, necessarily, at multidisciplinary colleges or universities.

- Free boarding facilities in the form of hostels will be built — matching the standard of Jawahar Navodaya Vidyalayas — in school locations where students may have to come from particularly far of places, anchor for students who come from disadvantaged economic backgrounds, with suitable arrangements for the safety of all children, especially girls (e.g., girls' hostels would be separate and secure and have female wardens, security guards, and boundary walls). Kasturba Gandhi Balika Vidyalayas will be strengthened and expanded to increase the participation in quality schools (up to Grade 12) of girls from socio-economically disadvantaged backgrounds. Additional Jawahar Navodaya Vidyalayas and Kendriya Vidyalayas will be built around the country, especially in aspiration districts, Special Education Zones and disadvantaged areas, to increase high-quality educational opportunities in every area of India. Pre-school sections will be added to Kendriya Vidyalayas and other primary schools around the nation, particularly in disadvantaged areas.

To conclude, it can be said in toto that a lot of policies are made with the best of intentions but only those which are effectively implemented are the ones which benefit any community. The NEP 2020 refers to the RPwD Act of 2016 at multiple points, be it when it defines Inclusive Education or benchmark disabilities but the reality is that the RPWD Act, 2016 itself is yet to be implemented in the country.

References

Anand, S. (2019). Online Education in India: Trends & Future Prospects, https://www.shiksha.com/mba/articles/ online-education-in-india-trends-future-prospects.

Drucker, P.F. (968): *The Age of Discontinuity: Guidelines to our Changing Society*. Heinemann: London.

Government of India (1986). *National Policy on Education*, Ministry of Education: New Delhi.

Government of India (1992) *The Programme on Action 1992 of National Policy on Education 1986,* Ministry of Education: New Delhi.

Government of India (2012). *Report to the people on Education,* 2011-12 MHRD: New Delhi.

Government of India (2011). All India Survey on Higher Education, MHRD.

Government of India (2020). The National Education Policy, MHRD: New Delhi https://mhrd.gov.in/sites/upload_file:///E:/EducationBook/NEP_Final_English.pdf.

Planning Commission (2007). *The Eleventh Five Year Plan 2007-2012* Vol. I, II & III Government of India: New Delhi.

Planning Commission (2013). *Twelfth Five Year Plan* 2012-17 Vol I, II & III. Government of India, Planning Commission: New Delhi.

Singha Roy, D.K. (2014). *Towards a Knowledge Society: New Identities in Emerging India.* Cambridge University Press: New Delhi.

UGC (2018). *Annual Report 2017-18.* UGC: New Delhi.

3

A Roadmap to Inclusive Education Vis-a-Vis National Education Policy 2020

Sonam Bansal (Dr.)*

Introduction

The goal of the National Education Policy 2020 is to expand educational opportunities for all. All children, including those with disabilities, should have access to school. An inclusive education is one in which both students and teachers collaborate to create and maintain a safe, supportive, and open-minded atmosphere. Inclusive classrooms are those in which consideration, mutual respect, and academic success are valued and fostered for all children. Inclusion should be practised irrespective of caste, colour, creed, economic inadequacy, sensorial, locomotory, and intellectual disability. In addition to promoting social inclusion, inclusive education eliminates prejudice and bullying. Over the years, the Government of India has enacted a number of educational rules, such as the RPwD Act of 2016 for inclusive education. Inequities remained despite the fact that every policy emphasized the child's access to formal education regardless of their background or skill level. The long-awaited National Education Policy has finally been established after 34 years. This paper will seek to explore the new provisional changes made to Inclusive Education in the NEP 2020. If we follow to the recommendations of NEP 2020, we might provide inclusive education to all children.

Education is essential to the growth and development of every civilization and should not be disregarded. A nation's potential could be squandered if its inhabitants do not have equal access to its resources. It is crucial to provide education to people from all walks of life so they can reach their greatest potential and live meaningful lives. The newly established National Education Policy (NEP) 2020 has taken many initiatives to expand access to higher education. In the next section, we shall examine how the NEP 2020 might assist India in developing a roadmap to educational inclusivity and potential.

In addition to teaching and assessment methods identified by disabled students (Ahmad, 2012), students have to have a library, notices, amusement

---

*Assistant Professor, Rao Lal Singh College of Education, Sidhrawali, Gurugram

outlets, sports facilities, and calendars. Curriculum, evaluation, infrastructure, transportation, emotional concerns, and teacher-student relationships also create problems. Higher education should give disabled students equal opportunities and more responsibility (Ahmad, 2016). UNESCO's four pillars of learning include "learning to live together" (Delors, 1996). In 2009, the UGC instructed that all central and state institutions build Disability Studies departments. Few Indian universities have these departments. RTE Act (2009) and RPwD Act (2016).

Despite better understanding, wider access, and Acts, India's situation is not improving to the desired level. After the NEP 2020 is revealed, difficulties and worries about including people with disabilities in higher education should be addressed. The policy discusses justice and inclusivity and recommends initiatives for colleges. Implementing a disabled strategy will be challenging. The institutions must develop a powerful committee for students with disabilities. This group will make sure disabled persons are not discriminated against in education and daily life. Universities should support inclusive education and college involvement. Certain criteria must be met to ensure that students accepted into higher education programmes will not dropout due to an unfavourable learning environment. Following aspects of the plan were employed to create a road map with timetables for disabled students in higher education.

- Conduct outreach on higher education opportunities and scholarships
- Make admission processes more inclusive
- Make curricula more inclusive
- Ensure all buildings are wheelchair accessible and disabled friendly
- Develop bridge courses for students that come from disadvantaged backgrounds
- Provide socio-emotional and academic support and mentoring
- Strictly enforce all no-discrimination and anti-harassment rules.

General Aspects of Roadmap to Inclusive Education vis-a-vis NEP 2020

The 2009 Right to Education Act (RTE) and the RPwD lack coherence on educational options for children with disabilities. The 2012 RTE Amendment lets children with disabilities attend neighbourhood schools and homeschools for those with severe disabilities. Students with qualifying impairments can attend neighbourhood or special schools. RTE and RPwD do not include special schools or homeschooling. The NEP aims to answer this issue by clearly declaring all three – neighbourhood schools, special schools, and home-based education – as choice for the education of children with disabilities, thereby attempting to resolve the ambiguities around school choice.

In order to fulfil the requirements of the NEP, inspections of home-based educational programmes will be carried out in accordance with the standards established by RPwD. It is imperative that a review of home-based education be carried out because there are questions regarding the process by which children are selected to participate in this provision and the standard of education that is given to them. When it comes to providing home-based education for special education students, teachers at the block level have mentioned a number of challenges they face. Limitations on time and resources, cultural norms and safety, and a lack of clear curriculum and examinations are some of the problems that must be overcome.

In spite of this, the provisions on education that are included in the RPwD place an emphasis on the establishment of a system of inclusive education. This is accomplished by the provision of accessible buildings and classrooms, in addition to individualized support that is geared toward full inclusion. The manner in which these laws are supposed to be applied in the context of home-based education, which is one of the educational paths that is not sponsored by the RPwD, is not completely clear. In addition, the endorsement of home-based education as an alternative to explaining how schools and classrooms can be made accessible and inclusive for children who have additional support needs raises questions about whether or not the educational system believes that some children with disabilities are unworthy of inclusion. Home-based education is an alternative to explaining how schools and classrooms can be made accessible and inclusive for children who have additional support needs.

According to the Requirements for People with Disabilities Act (RPwD), children who are eligible for special education under the NEP will be offered the chance to attend specialised schools. Despite the recent rebranding of the Ministry of Education, it is not yet clear whether the newly renamed Ministry of Education will govern special schools in the same manner as ordinary schools or whether they will continue to fall under the purview of the Ministry of Social Justice and Welfare. This is despite the fact that the Ministry of Education has recently undergone a rebranding, Social Justice and Empowerment (MSJE). When special schools are not recognised as legitimate educational institutions because there are no defined regulations on quality, curriculum, certification, or infrastructure, it is unfair to children with disabilities who attend those schools. It lends credence to the idea that some pupils should attend schools that are segregated along racial lines rather than having a single educational system that serves all students. As a direct consequence of this division, the "social inclusion toward a benign model of social isolation" undergoes further transformation.

The RPwD has a limited authority to enforce standards, so the current procedures for regulating special schools are typically insufficient. This is one of the reasons why special schools are commonly under regulated. Education authorities are the only ones that have the authority to strip schools of their recognition if they fail to meet certain conditions. As a direct consequence of this, the progressive measures outlined in the NEP for students who have disabilities may or may not be applicable to special schools. For instance, it is extremely unlikely that information on the facilities, resources, and educational expectations of special schools will be made available to the general public.

The NEP said these components will help regular schools become "vibrant institutions of excellence." It is unclear if this would apply to deaf schools, which emphasize lip-reading and speech therapy above sign language. The Ministry of Education does not oversee special schools. Deaf schools usually teach lip-reading and speech therapy more than sign language. National Education Policy supports standardization of Indian Sign Language for hard-of-hearing children. The position of special schools within the inclusive education policy framework is uncertain.

The NEP makes school choice for disabled children more difficult by implementing school complexes and rationalization programmes. All schools within a 5- to 10-kilometer radius of the proposed complex will be integrated. According to the document, this will ensure that there are enough resource centers and special educators for children with disabilities. This is an attempt to solve a major problem for disabled children: the chronic shortage of special educators. Block-level special educators often serve students from more than 150 schools and travel far to serve all disabled children in their blocks.

Parents prioritise school proximity. Disabled children's parents worry about public transit safety. In certain areas, mothers accompany their children to school to protect their safety and well-being, while paying all associated costs. Children with high support needs and their attendants do not get their RPwD transportation allowance or services. In an effort to rationalize resources and provide more individualized services and assistance, school complexes may restrict disabled students' attendance and enrollment. These are challenges for school complexes. Disabled children may be segregated in schools and resource centres. These children may be pulled from class.

By implementing the RPwD definition of inclusive education, the NEP differentiates between social justice, education for all, and a system where students with and without disabilities learn together. The NEP fails to clarify "inclusion" and "integration" in Indian education.

Education policies in India have historically used inclusion and integration interchangeably without recognizing key differences and continuing practices that require disabled children to adjust and fit within the system (integration) rather than transforming core practices to be truly equitable and inclusive. NEP uses inclusion, integration, mitigation, rehabilitation, disability, divyang, special needs children, and differently abled. This is not a word choice issue; it is the incoherence of the Indian educational system. NEP conflates special education. The policy regards disability as a problem to be 'rehabilitated' and 'mitigated' to help disabled children 'integrate'. It allows children with and without disabilities to be in the same classroom, addresses barrier-free access, and incorporates handicapped children in curriculum and evaluation. These are retrofitting remedies to the 'problem of disability', not a critical assessment of albeit practices. It opposes inclusive education, which views disabilities as systemic, not human, shortcomings.

Peer tutoring, open schooling, and one-on-one education are provided to disabled children. Standardizing Indian Sign Linguistics would be an example of recognizing disability as an identity and a variation rather than a weakness. Difficult curriculum, inaccessible schools and classrooms, lack of customized evaluations, and deficit attitudes hamper disabled children's success.

India joined the UNCRPD in 2007, which provides all disabled children a free, quality education. According to the UNCRPD, the NEP must lead to increased financial allocation, a systems approach, and cross-government collaboration.

National Education Policy 2020 – Goals

The National Education Policy 2020 is an initiative that encourages inclusive education and equal access to high-quality education for all students, irrespective of gender, caste, creed, religious affiliation, or socio-economic status. The goal of this initiative is to realise the vision of the National Education Policy by the year 2020. The following primary considerations are outlined in the policy with regard to the provision of education that is available to all children.

Every child has the right to free and obligatory education up until the age of 14, regardless of whether or not they have special needs. This includes the right for children with special needs to acquire education.

There shall be no discrimination in the process of admission to educational institutions based on the socio-economic position of a candidate's or applicant's family. This includes both public and private schools.

Those who are disadvantaged or marginalised, such as members of SC/ST communities, members of minority groups, and women, will receive special attention.

Educational institutions will make the infrastructure and support workers that are necessary for accommodating children who have special needs available, which will result in educational institutions becoming more inclusive. This will allow educational institutions to accommodate children who have special needs.

Inclusive education will be incorporated into the curricula of schools at all levels, beginning with early childhood care and education and continuing all the way through higher education. This will be done in order to ensure that all students have equal access to learning opportunities.

Education

NEP 2020 supports each and every suggestion made by the RPwD Act 2016 with reference to education. Giving children with disabilities frequent educational opportunities from early childhood through higher education has been given significant attention by the approach. Children with moderate to severe disabilities will have the option of regular or special schooling.

Complex School

The school complex will house a resource centre in addition to other services. Additionally, the school must guarantee that special educators with cross-disability training are hired. The school will get assistance in order to create customised adjustments and support mechanisms in order to meet the needs of the child with a disability and to ensure barrier-free access.

Curriculum, Assistive Technology, and Supportive Technology

NCERT will cooperate with specialised organisations like DEPwD to provide a national curriculum framework (NEP 2020, Part-I, Section 6.10). NIOS is in charge of developing top-notch modules to teach Indian Sign Language and other basic disciplines. Students will be able to work at their own pace because the curriculum can be modified based on their ability. In order to integrate and immerse the child in the classroom activities, the required technology-based tools, different assistive equipment, and appropriate, language-appropriate teaching-learning resources, such as Braille and large print textbooks, will be made available in school.

Teacher

NEP 2020 discusses reforming teacher education programmes. Programmes for teacher preparation should include sensitivity training, early intervention, support, and special pedagogy to teach students with disabilities.

Analysis

For the evaluation of children with disabilities, the National Assessment Centre, PARAKH, will create the regulations and make instrumental suggestions. All tests, including admission tests, from the elementary school level to higher education will be affected by this.

Discussion

The New Education Policy is an all-encompassing strategy. It consists of all the elements necessary for the full integration of disabled children into the educational system. The five elements that follow are an effort to structure all the ideas in NEP 2020.

Positive Mentality

One of the biggest obstacles to inclusion is attitude. Teachers, who are the foundation of the educational system, can influence students' attitudes toward inclusive education. For this, teachers need to be well-trained for inclusion as well as sensitive to inclusion. In order to instill the principles and competencies necessary for inclusive education, NEP 2020 discusses changes to the teacher education curriculum.

School Readiness

The success of inclusive education depends on how well-equipped the school is to meet the needs of the disabled students. NEP 2020 places a high premium on school readiness. The components of a school's readiness for inclusion include the establishment of resource centres throughout each complex of schools, the hiring of special educators, and specialised support services.

Resources and Assistance

Each student must have access to the necessary resources in the school, including supportive and assistive technology, which has a very thorough plan in place for assisting the NEP. Both the school and the parents of homeschoolers are supported by the resource centre. For a child to receive a high-quality education, the state must support both the school and the parents. NEP 2020 also includes orientation workshops for parents who are homeschooling their children.

Personalized Programme

Like no two children are alike, neither are any two children with disabilities. As a result, each challenged child has distinct needs depending on their disability. The secret to success in designing an educational programme for these children are that no one design fits all.

According to the NEP 2020, the school must offer these kids specialised programmes.

Flexible Education

We are unable to force these kids to learn what their peers are learning since they have quite different needs and abilities than their peers. And for the sake of these kids, a flexible curriculum and flexible evaluation methods are very necessary. In addition to discussing customizable curricula, NEP 2020 also mentions PARAKH for simple assessment. NCERT and DEPwD will collaborate to build the national curricular framework, according to NEP 2020.

Conclusion

This roadmap will serve as an essential foundation upon which to construct, as the supply of education that is available to each and every one of India's people has been an ongoing struggle for the country. If we stick to the standards that are outlined in NEP 2020, we will be able to create educational opportunities for all children that are more inclusive for them. This will allow us to better meet the needs of all children. The children's backgrounds and the criteria they have will not make a difference; this will always be the case. In addition, in order to foster genuine acceptance and comprehension, it is of the utmost importance that our communities go through significant cultural shifts in regard to how people with disabilities should be viewed and how they should talk about them. This is because these shifts are necessary in order to cultivate genuine acceptance and comprehension. This is due to the fact that these transformations are essential in order to cultivate real acceptance and comprehension of one another. If we adhere to the plan that has been laid out for us, we will be able to make progress toward our goal of establishing an educational system that is egalitarian and enables people to develop regardless of where they came from. This can be accomplished if we follow the roadmap that has been laid out for us.

References

Bairwa, S.L. (n.d.). National Educational Policy 2020 with special reference to the inclusive and quality based higher education. *International Journal of Health Sciences*. Retrieved January 5, 2023, from https://doi.org/10.53730/ijhs.v6nS6.10051

Electronic Journal for inclusive education - wright State University. (n.d.). Retrieved January 5, 2023, from https://corescholar.libraries.wright.edu/cgi/viewcontent.cgi?article=1086 &context=ejie *(PDF) A roadmap to inclusive education in NEP2020 - Researchgate*. (n.d.). Retrieved January 5, 2023, from https://www.researchgate.net/publication/348364008_A_Roadmap_to_In clusive_Education_in_NEP2020

India's new education policy (NEP) 2020: Catering for children with ... (n.d.). Retrieved January 5, 2023, from https://www.researchgate.net/profile/Deep-Kumar-9/publication/358451339_India's_New_Education_Policy_NEP_2020_Catering_for_Children_with_Disabilities/links/620314e40445354498d21b 79/Indias-New-Education-Policy-NEP-2020-Catering-for-Children-with-Disabilities.pdf

National educational policy 2020 with special reference to the ... (n.d.). Retrieved January 5, 2023, from https://www.researchgate.net/publication/362143354_National_education al_policy_2020_with_special_reference_to_the_inclusive_and_quality_b ased_higher_education

Perceived opportunities of national education policy-2020. (n.d.). Retrieved January 5, 2023, from https://www.researchgate.net/publication/363739105_Perceived_Opportu nities_of_National_Education_Policy-2020

Political participation of women in India: Problems and prospects. (n.d.). Retrieved January 4, 2023, from https://www.researchgate.net/publication/352814150_Political_Participati on_Of_Women_In_India_Problems_And_Prospects

4

National Education Policy 2020
A Critical Assessment

Ritu Arora (Dr.)*

Introduction

> *"As the Island of Knowledge grows, so do the shores of our ignorance — the boundary between the known and unknown .... The more we know, the more exposed we are to our ignorance, and the more we know to ask".*
>
> (Gleiser, 2014)

Education is fundamental to human survival and growth (Sianesi & Reenen, 2003). It is a continuous process that is lifelong for an individual while spanning generations for society as a whole. A phenomenon with such pervasive permanence is bound to arouse interest among psychologists, civil society, and policy-makers (Dill, 1997; Nicholson-Crotty & Meier, 2003). Within this realm, National Education Policy document (NEP 2020), released by the Ministry of Education, Government of India, is a welcome initiative. It has to be seen as a well-intentioned move to steer India and its demographic dividend into a world that thrives on knowledge and information as its pillars of development (Chandrasekhar et al., 2006). However, the success of any public policy is seldom driven by documentary idealism. What is additionally required is an understanding and management of practical challenges and implementation resolve (Ingrams et al., 2020).

The objective of this work is thus simply to put NEP 2020 to the test of how the roadmap it charts maps to its goals. Government investment in education is vital in a diverse context like our country. My intention throughout this work is not to find loopholes in what the government proposes to do. Instead, it is to draw attention to some of the areas which need more attention from the policy-makers and contribute in a minor way as a citizen to better education of our children.

What is it? A Vision Document, A Framework or A Detailed Programme of Action?

Is NEP 2020a vision document that specifies some ideals, a state of existence that we want to reach as a nation in the context of education? If so, we should

*Assistant Professor, Khalsa College of Education, G.T. Road, Amritsar

be more concerned with the long-term goals that we aspire to achieve. Further, in that case, it is definitionally immune to critiques that ask for implementation roadmaps. A second possibility is it being a framework, a modular combination of aims, existing and proposed practices, that has the potential to commence the transformation of our educational system while specificities manifest and are ironed out on the path. Third, it may be categorised as an elaborate document detailing the policy interventions and initiatives envisioned of different actors. In that case, it is a more comprehensive policy document that supplements goals with the exact roadmap.

A neutral reading of the NEP 2020 document is more likely to view it as the second form, i.e., at the most, a framework with many loose ends that need to be thought of and assimilated. Several analyses of the NEP 2020 put forward this view of it as a skeleton, where the flesh (e.g., plan of action) and blood (e.g., resources) are largely missing, at least currently (Govinda, 2020; Menon, 2020). To its credit, the NEP 2020 incorporates most facets of education, including language, literacy, teacher motivation, curriculum, autonomy, and empowerment. Still, it falls short on documenting the ways and means of the transformation it envisions.

Goals

National Education Policy 2020 structures its aims in four heads, that of school education, higher education, other key areas of focus, and making it happen. First, NEP 2020 emphasises the foundational phase of a child's education through its early childhood care and education (ECCE) focus. Moving from the current 10+2 system, which relatively exogenises the child's learning before Ist standard/ six-year age to the informal mechanisms, the proposed 5+3+3+4 system recognises the importance of the formative phase when a child is in the 3-6 years age group. The NEP 2020 then aims at achieving universal foundational literacy and numeracy for all primary school children by 2025. Curtailing dropout rates and ensuring universal access is another goal within school education, and the NEP 2020 expresses particular concern about the IXth and Xth standards, which are outside the ambit of the RTE Act. It also aims to adapt the *curriculum and pedagogy* to the proposed 5+3+3+4 design, striving for holistic development of pupils based on reduced syllabi, flexibility, critical thinking, experiential learning, multilingualism, and changed modes of assessment. It aims to expand teacher recruitment and deployment on the soft infrastructure front, complementing it with enabling service environment, career progression, professional development and standardisation, and continuing training. NEP 2020 also aims to carry forward the agenda of equitable and inclusive education, including expanding the socio-economically disadvantaged citizen groups targeted under current government interventions. Finally, it envisages better governance and accreditation systems for the school education structure of the country.

For the higher education sector, NEP 2020 aims to improve the quality of universities and colleges through institutional restructuring and consolidation, holistic and multidisciplinary education, optimal learning environment and support, internationalisation, motivated and capable faculty, equity and inclusion, teacher education, vocational education, research, and transformation of the regulatory system. It also aims to curb *commercialisation* and improve the *governance* of higher education institutions (HEIs).

Working on professional education and toward adult and lifelong learning are some of its other focus areas. Blending learning with Indian *languages, arts, and culture* is seen as vital to preserving our rich heritage and improving outcomes. At the same time, modernisation, including extensive use of *technology*, offering online and digital delivery programmes, and creating digital infrastructure and content, is also emphasised.

Roadmap

From the perspective of its aims, NEP 2020 is unequivocally a well-crafted document. However, there are doubts about whether the world it envisions is too idealistic, separated enormously from the handicaps of the real educational institutions and their targeted learners (Govinda, 2020). With the emphasis on ECCE, one of the central and most transformational areas, NEP 2020 proposes the expansion and strengthening of the Anganwadi system, opening new preschools, and co-location of both entities with existing primary schools. There is no mention of the resources that would be required for such an exercise. Further, there is no projection even of the number of such centres that could suffice for our nation. Similarly, it talks of teacher additions and their continuing training without mentioning the specific plan of action that could be adopted. There is a parallel lack of clarity on how basic literacy and numeracy outcomes would be improved, given that efforts to improve the teaching quality have already been going on for years (Kumar & Wiseman, 2021). For example, stringent recruitment checks like teacher eligibility tests (Govinda, 2016), also one of the proposed initiatives under this goal is setting up school libraries in each village. How are resources supposed to be generated for this, when many schools still do not have toilets (Chatterjee et al., 2018)? The broader goal of equity and inclusive education and its roadmap is discussed separately under the 'Public Investment' sub-section.

Under the higher education sector, NEP 2020 wants to set up at least one multidisciplinary HEI in or near every district. However, it does not specify, how such a goal maps to the current or planned expansion of state-funded HEIs. Correspondingly, there is no linkage to approvals granted or private-sector HEIs already in the pipeline. NEP 2020 also aims to improve quality by enhancing the autonomy of HEIs and improving regulation/accreditation systems. Such ideas again appear lofty ideals relative to the current position where governments across states and the centre appear to be intruding into the academic space via deciding syllabi, recruitments, promotions, etc. (Carnoy & Dossani, 2013).

Another vital aspect is that education is on the concurrent list (Panchamukhi, 2013). There could be little movement on the ground unless states are entirely on board. Nowhere does NEP recognise the need to clarify how states will be convinced or incentivised. Almost all central government programmes, irrespective of the sector, involve shared expenditure from states and also incorporate means of similar devolution of generated resources, if any (Mooij & Dev, 2004). However, NEP 2020 assumes away all regional and contextual differences in dreaming of a pan-India footprint.

In summary, thus, NEP 2020 does not sufficiently recognise the entrenched nature of the present education system, its infrastructure, norms, mindsets of current stakeholders, etc. That we are already a republic running into its eighth decade and not an infant nation with a clean slate is something that cannot be easily ignored.

Public Investment

Health and education are sectors where even the most ardent admirers of the market economy accept the government's critical role (Gupta et al., 2002; Hendren & Sprung-Keyser, 2020). Successive Indian governments have incorporated this emphasis in their development narratives. Still, spending on these sectors as a percentage of the Indian GDP has remained stagnant (Guruswamy et al., 2008). Simultaneously and to some extent resultingly, we see a gradual decline in the public health and education systems. NEP 2020 falls shy of enumerating the specifics of how public investment in education would be maintained, much less expanded. It is unclear how its aim of almost doubling the gross enrolment ratio (GER) in higher education by 2035 can be achieved in a system where most of the funding goes to premier institutes like IITs and IIMs, whereas most of the student enrolment is with other higher education institutions (HEIs) like state universities (Menon, 2020). The policy's appeal for *private philanthropic efforts* may not yield much, given the ever-increasing commercialisation of the sector, right from the pre-school stage to the university phase. More worryingly, a push to increase the student numbers (GER) in the current set-up has the adverse potential of pushing the already burdened HEIs into a state of chronic starvation.

Conclusion

Human beings are naturally endowed with, arguably, the best mental faculties among living beings. Still, it is universally accepted that education is the oil that prevents this potential from rusting. Like with most social phenomena, not all educational interventions are equally effective (Conn, 2017; Hattie, Biggs, & Purdie, 1996), nor is the learning outcome (quantitative as well as qualitative) of each intervention uniform across learners (Biggs, 1979; Jonassen & Grabowski, 2012; Schiefele, 1991).

It is, thus, vital to take an objective and informed position on the ways and means of imparting education. Educators and policy-makers need to understand all components of the learning process, including how individuals learn (Cassidy, 2004). At the same time, the vastness of the educational process forces us to limit our focus to parts at a time rather than a singular look at its totality (Kansanen, 2003). This work thus has taken a restricted look at the contours of the proposed NEP 2020 and presented some points for policy-makers to refine the content and implementation roadmap of the same.

References

Biggs, J. (1979). Individual differences in study processes and the quality of learning outcomes. *Higher Education, 8*(4), 381–394.

Carnoy, M., & Dossani, R. (2013). Goals and governance of higher education in India. *Higher Education, 65*(5), 595-612.

Cassidy, S. (2004). Learning styles: An overview of theories, models, and measures. *Educational Psychology, 24*(4), 419–444.

Chandrasekhar, C.P., Ghosh, J., & Roychowdhury, A. (2006). The demographic dividend and young India's economic future. *Economic and Political Weekly*, 5055–5064.

Chatterjee, I., Li, I., & Robitaille, M.C. (2018). An overview of India's primary school education policies and outcomes 2005–2011. *World Development, 106*, 99-110.

Conn, K.M. (2017). Identifying effective education interventions in sub-Saharan Africa: A meta-analysis of impact evaluations. *Review of Educational Research, 87*(5), 863–898.

Dill, D.D. (1997). Higher education markets and public policy. *Higher Education Policy, 10*(3–4), 167–185.

Gleiser, M. (2014). *The island of knowledge: The limits of science and the search for meaning*. Basic Books.

Govinda, R. (2016). Transforming Indian school education: Policy concerns and Priorities. *Yojana, 60*(1), 7-10.

Govinda, R. (2020). NEP 2020: A critical examination. *Social Change, 50*(4), 603-607.

Gupta, S., Verhoeven, M., & Tiongson, E.R. (2002). The effectiveness of government spending on education and health care in developing and transition economies. *European Journal of Political Economy, 18*(4), 717-737.

Guruswamy, M., Mazumdar, S., & Mazumdar, P. (2008). Public financing of health services in India: an analysis of central and state government expenditure. *Journal of Health Management, 10*(1), 49-85.

Hattie, J., Biggs, J., & Purdie, N. (1996). Effects of learning skills interventions on student learning: A meta-analysis. *Review of Educational Research, 66*(2), 99–136.

Hendren, N., & Sprung-Keyser, B. (2020). A unified welfare analysis of government policies. *The Quarterly Journal of Economics, 135*(3), 1209-1318.

Ingrams, A., Piotrowski, S., & Berliner, D. (2020). Learning from our mistakes: Public management reform and the hope of open government. *Perspectives on Public Management and Governance*, *3*(4), 257–272.

Jonassen, D.H., & Grabowski, B.L. (2012). *Handbook of individual differences, learning, and instruction*. Routledge.

Kansanen, P. (2003). Studying – the realistic bridge between instruction and learning. An attempt to a conceptual whole of the teaching-studying-learning process. *Educational Studies*, *29*(2–3), 221–232.

Kumar, P., & Wiseman, A.W. (2021). Teacher quality discourse in India: A national reform agenda content analysis. *Teaching and Teacher Education*, *107*, 103504.

Menon, S. (2020). NEP 2020: Some Searching Questions. *Social Change*, *50*(4), 599-602.

Mooij, J., & Dev, S.M. (2004). Social sector priorities: an analysis of budgets and expenditures in India in the 1990s. *Development Policy Review*, *22*(1), 97-120.

Nicholson-Crotty, J., & Meier, K.J. (2003). Politics, structure, and public policy: The case of higher education. *Educational Policy*, *17*(1), 80–97.

Panchamukhi, P.R. (2013). Education and Federalism in India. *The Indian Economic Journal*, *60*(4), 174-178.

Schiefele, U. (1991). Interest, learning, and motivation. *Educational Psychologist*, *26*(3–4), 299–323.

Sianesi, B., & Reenen, J.V. (2003). The returns to education: Macroeconomics. *Journal of Economic Surveys*, *17*(2), 157–200.

5

Inclusive Education Vis-à-Vis National Education Policy 2020

Neerja Gautam (Dr.)*

Introduction

> "A nation is advanced in proportion to education and intelligence spread among the masses".
>
> Swami Vivekananda

An estimated 240 million children worldwide live with disabilities. Like all children, children with disabilities have ambitions and dreams for their futures. Like all children, they need quality education to develop their skills and realise their full potential.

Yet, children with disabilities are often overlooked in policymaking, limiting their access to education and their ability to participate in social, economic and political life. Worldwide, these children are among the most likely to be out of school. They face persistent barriers to education stemming from discrimination, stigma and the routine failure of decision makers to incorporate disability in school services.

Education denotes that all children irrespective of their strengths and weaknesses will be part of the mainstream education. It is clear that education policies in India has gradually increased the focus on children and adults with special needs, and that inclusive education in regular schools has become a primary policy objective.

The definition of inclusive education is given by UNESCO's Section for Special Needs Education (UNESCO, 2000) as, "Inclusive education is concerned with removing all barriers to learning, and with the participation of all learners vulnerable to exclusion and marginalisation. It is a strategic approach designed to facilitate learning success for all children. It addresses the common goals of decreasing and overcoming all exclusion from the human right to education, at least at the elementary level, and enhancing access, participation and learning success in quality basic education for all."

* Associate Professor, DAV College of Education for Women, Amritsar

Inclusive education is a new approach towards educating the children with disability and learning difficulties with that of normal ones within the same roof. It brings all students together in one classroom and community, regardless of their strengths or weaknesses in any area, and seeks to maximise the potential of all students. It is one of the most effective ways to promote an inclusive and tolerant society. It is known that 73 million children of primary school age were out of school in 2010, down from a high of over 110 million out of school children in the mid-1990s, according to new estimates by the UNESCO Institute for Statistics (UIS). About 80% of Indian population lives in rural areas without provisions for special schools. It means, there are an estimated eight million children out of school in India (MHRD, 2009 statistics), many of whom are marginalised by dimensions such as poverty, gender, disability and caste.

Therefore, inclusive schools have to address the needs of all children in every community and the central and state governments have to manage inclusive classrooms. There is a need to place inclusive education within a common framework which will provide important tools for planning, collaboration and implementation of the principles of NEP 2020 in a systematic manner. In the year 2015, India adopted the 2030 agenda for sustainable development. The goal 4 of SDG mentioned to "ensure inclusive and equitable quality education and promote lifelong learning opportunities for all" by 2030 (NEP, 2020).

An Overview of Inclusive Education in India

1) In India, the Kothari Education Commission (1964-66) emphasised on the need for development of an effective education programme for the people with disability, to ensure the equalisation of educational opportunities.
2) The first education policy of India was introduced in 1968 on the recommendation of Kothari Education Commission.
3) NPE 1968 pronounced "Educational facilities for the physically and mentally handicapped children should be expanded, and attempts should be made to develop integrated programmes enabling the handicapped children to study in mainstream schools" (NPE, 1968).
4) A programme for Integrated Education was included in the Planning Commission of India in the year 1971.
5) In December 1974, a scheme named Integrated Education for Disabled Children (IEDC), was launched by Government of India in order to put the idea of integration into action. The vision of this scheme was to promote integration of the children who have mild or moderate disabilities in the regular schools.
6) In the year 1976 education was added in the concurrent list by the 42nd amendment.

7) Article 45 was introduced in 1949. Article 45 ensures the free and compulsory education for all children from age 6 to 14 years.
8) The second education policy of India was adopted in 1986. NPE 1986 by emphasising on Inclusive Education states that "the children with mild disabilities should be permitted to education in the regular school while the children with moderate to severe disabilities should continue to get education in the special school" (NPE, 1986).
9) In the year 1987, the Mental Health Act came into action which revoked the Indian Lunacy Act of 1912 intending to consolidate the law for mentally ill persons.
10) In the same year, the Project Integrated Education for the Disabled (PIED) to encourage the school in the neighborhood to enroll the children with disabilities was introduced. This was a joint venture of Education Ministry with NCERT and UNICEF.
11) However, the Programme of Action in the year 1992, stated that "the children disabilities who can be integrated in the regular school must get education there and the children who are facing problem in integrating in the regular school must send to the special schools. After learning skills, they can further be shifted to the regular school" (POA, 1992).
12) Rehabilitation Council of India Act (RCI) also came in September 1992. This Act was enforced for regulating the training of rehabilitation professionals and the maintenance of a Central Rehabilitation Register.
13) After RCI Act the Persons with Disabilities Act came in 1995, which ensures the full participation and equality of the people with disabilities in the Asian and Pacific Region.
14) With the joint effort of Government of India and the World Bank in 1997, the District Primary Education Program was launched. DPEP states that "any difference that a child exhibited in learning was to be attributed not a problem with child, but of school system." This was the first time when the emphasis was on the school preparedness (DPEP, 1997).
15) In the year 1999, National Trust for Welfare of Persons with Autism, Cerebral Palsy, Mental Retardation and Multiple Disabilities Act came. To provide financial support to the people with mentioned four disabilities, various schemes such as "Reach and Relief Scheme" and "Samarth Scheme" was introduced (National Trust Act, 1999).
16) For the Universalisation of Elementary Education, Government of India launched Sarva Shiksha Abhiyan (SSA) in 2001. Though SSA was not an intervention specific to disability but the emphasis was Education for All.
17) In the year 2009, Inclusive Education of the Disabled at the Secondary Stage (IEDSS) was introduced. This was a reformed of IEDC for secondary stage education.

18) In the same year Rastriya Madhyamik Shiksha Abhiyan (RMSA) was introduced by the Government of India, for the Universalisation of Secondary Education.
19) 2009 was a major year in education for India. The Right to Education Act was passed in the same year and enforced from 1 April 2010. RTE 2009 under the Article 21A makes the education a fundamental right of every child in India.
20) The Rights of Person with Disability Act 2016, replaced the PwD Act of 1995. This act was in line with the UNCRPD. It includes 21 conditions as disable. The central and state government will establish advisory board on disability.
21) In the year 2018, the Samagra Shiksha Abhiyan was launched by the MHRD. It is an integrated scheme for school education, which merged three scheme SSA (Sarva Shiksha Abhiyan), RMSA (Rastriya Madhyamik Shiksha Abhiyan) and TE (Teacher Education).

Inclusive Education in National Education Policy 2020

Based on the recommendation given by the Kasturirangan Committee (2019), the National Education Policy has been launched after 34 years. This is a very comprehensive policy covering all the levels of education. The policy spread into four parts. Equitable and inclusive education is covered under school education (NEP, 2020).

While the policy does lay emphasis on gender sensitisation, what needs more attention is the curriculum. The component of sex education needs to be carefully added and be made a mandatory part of the teaching-learning process. The National Education Policy (NEP) 2020 envisages equitable and inclusive education for all, with special focus on children and youth, especially girls, from socially and economically disadvantaged groups. The policy's focus is important because despite effort to educate women, the dropout rate for girls is still high after secondary education. The enrolment ratio too dips at the secondary and higher secondary levels. Among many reasons, the onset of menstruation and the lack of availability of hygienic toilets are responsible for girls leaving school without completing education. The NEP 2020 intends to meet this challenge through its Gender Inclusion Fund (GIF). The fund will be used to provide quality education to all students.

NEP 2020 aims to address the issue of gender inequity in recruitment of teachers in rural areas. The policy hopes to adopt new methods that will ensure that merit and qualifications are taken into consideration and that women teachers are provided appropriate forums for recruitment. It is a fact that sound teacher training is imperative for quality education.

The policy has underlined the necessity for teachers and facilitators like anganwadi workers to undergo proper training to counsel the families of girl students. This inclusion of the family for counseling is significant as the gap between an educated girl child and her uneducated family leads to a different set of problems.

A definite way forward for girl students would be the skill enhancement courses that NEP foregrounds. Economic empowerment of women through skilling in educational institutions will surely be progressive and attract girl students to educational institutions as well as, hopefully, change the way that traditionally families distinguish between male/female education, seeing the former as a more rewarding proposition.

While the policy does lay emphasis on gender sensitisation, what needs more attention is the curriculum. The component of sex education needs to be carefully added and be made a mandatory part of the teaching-learning process. This should include instruction on menstrual health and hygiene.

Another important aspect that should be included as compulsory education is legal literacy. The girl student must be aware of her legal rights. Framers of curriculum under NEP 2020 must ensure that these two essential domains are properly factored into the curriculum and not done as tokenism with mere cosmetic value.

Furthermore, female health should be of prime importance and care should be taken that the right kind of nutrition is provided to female students; the mid day meal, or even the breakfast as mentioned in NEP, in themselves good initiatives of the government, are not enough to battle malnourishment faced by female students.

The New Education Policy is a comprehensive plan. It includes all those aspects that will lead to full inclusion of the children with disability in the education system. The following five aspects are an attempt to give a structure to all the points included in NEP 2020.

- *Positive Attitude* — Attitude is one of the most significant barriers to inclusion. Teacher as a pillar of the education system can bring a positive attitude among students towards inclusive education. This requires the teachers not only to be sensitised towards inclusion but also well trained for the inclusion. NEP 2020 talks about the reforms in teacher education programme to inculcate the values and skills required for inclusive education.
- *School Preparedness* — Inclusive education can only be successful if the school is well prepared to cater to the needs of the children with disability. NEP 2020 gives priority to the school preparedness. Resource centre in every school complex and recruitment of the special educators and the individualised support programmes are the aspects of school readiness towards inclusion.
- *Resources and Support* — Assistive, supportive device and other resources according to the individual needs must be available in the school. When

it comes to supporting NEP 2020 has a very detailed plan. The resource centre supports not only the school but also the home-schooling parents. The school and the parents must be provided support by the state for quality education. Orientation programmes for the parents providing home-schooling are also a part of NEP 2020.

- *Individualised Programme* — No two children are alike similarly, no two disabled children are alike. So, for every disabled child with different disabilities have diverse needs. No one size fits all is the key to success here when it comes to design educational programme for these children. NEP 2020 has the provision of the school to provide individualised programmes for these children.
- *Flexible Curriculum* — These children have very distinct need and ability than their peers and that is why we cannot make them learn whatever their peers are learning. And that is why a flexible curriculum and a flexible assessment mechanism is very much essential for the betterment of these children. NEP 2020 not only talked about the flexible curriculum but also talk about PARAKH for easy assessment. NEP 2020 also mentioned, for the development of national curriculum framework NCERT will work along with PEDwD.

Only placement of the child with disability will not help. If we want to grow as a country, it is our moral duty to make education accessible to every child regardless of their disability. India as a country of diversity, always see these diversities as an opportunity similarly, now it is time that the mindset of people to change and see every disability as a special ability. That is to focus on what these children can do better rather than merely focusing on things that they cannot do. From segregation to inclusion, the inclusive education system in India goes through several hurdles. To look at the disability as a special ability, it's required a change in the mindset. Finally, the government of India came up with such a policy which include the minute details. At the school level, teachers must be trained, buildings must be refurnished and students must receive accessible learning materials. At the community level, stigma and discrimination must be tackled and individuals need to be educated on the benefit of inclusive education. At the national level, governments must align laws and policies with the Convention on the Rights of Persons with Disabilities, and regularly collect and analyse data to ensure children are enriched with effective services.

Conclusion

"All of us do not have equal talent. But, all of us have an equal opportunity to develop our talents".

Dr. A P J Abdul Kalam

References

Panigrahi, Soumya Priyadarsani and Malik, Navita (2020). A roadmap to inclusive education in NEP 2020. *Juni Khyat* Vol-10 Issue-10 No. 03 October 2020

Singh, J.D. (2016) Inclusive education in India — concept, need and challenges. *Scholarly Research Journal For Humanity Science & English Language, Dec-Jan, 2016, vol. 3/13 www.srjis.com*

https://www.hindustantimes.com/opinion/nep-2020-making-education-gender-inclusive-101646724488825.html retrieved on 08 July 2022

https://www.unicef.org/education/inclusive-education

Rajaraman and Krishna (2021). Inclusive education for children with disabilities during COVID-19.http://idronline.org>Education

6

Inclusive Education in India
Policy Provisions and Challenges

Raminder Kaur*

Introduction

Indian society is naturally more inclusive than segregationist in nature. Starting from Gurukul system to western model of day-care system, efforts have been made to bring people in, rather than to keep them out. An integration of students with disabilities into general education classrooms indicates that all children irrespective of their strengths and weaknesses shall be a part of the mainstream education. The feeling of belongingness among all teachers, students and other functionaries is envisaged through inclusive education. Every child is special for his/her parent and every child has a special need for love, acceptance and a feeling of belongingness. India is a signatory to the United Nations Standard Rules on Equalization of Opportunities, the Jomtien Declaration on Education for All and the Salamanca Statement and Framework for Action. In this paper an attempt has been made to look at the importance and challenges for the execution of inclusive education in India

Conceptualizing Inclusive Education

Inclusive education is a new approach for educating the disabled children or children with special needs along with the normal ones at the same place. It emphasizes on the provision of equal opportunity for people with disability claiming for participation and equality for all. It addresses the learning needs of children with a specific focus on those who are vulnerable to learn together in the same school, or community. The principle of inclusive education was adopted at the "World Conference on Special Needs Education: Access and Quality" (Salamanca, Spain 1994) and was restated at the World Education Forum (Dakar, Senegal 2000). Inclusive education is not a test but a value which helps in educating people with or without disability altogether. With the inheritance of inclusive education in India, more than 90% of children with disability were provided with education which helped them in becoming financially

*Assistant Professor, Khalsa College of Education, G.T. Road, Amritsar

independent and grow in the life. With the support initiated by United Nation's Standard Rules on Equalization of opportunities for person with disability, Indian educational system also imbibed inclusive education in its curriculum. Inclusive education is one in which children in special schools were shifted to one where the whole school was encouraged to become more adaptable and inclusive in its day-to-day educational practices for all students.

Importance of Inclusive Education

Education is indeed the most effective tool to attain social and economic empowerment. Inclusive education can play a paramount role in enabling disabled persons to live successful lives. It is not only necessary to support such children in their academic activities, but it is also necessary to promote their overall growth and development. They should also be motivated to participate in extracurricular activities such as dance, music, painting, drawing, craft and other creative work (Kacker, 2013). Differently abled children also have equal right to get education as per their needs and capability. Every stakeholder of the society has to understand his/her roles and responsibilities to work with cooperation and coherence to ensure that not a single child is left without school education. Differently abled children should be treated equally as the normal children and instead of looking at them in sympathy their talents and abilities should be recognized for their self-respect and welfare of the society. Government of India is trying to improve its education system focusing on the inclusive approach. With the initiation of Article 21, Indian constitution has also made education as the fundamental basic right of every individual and Article 15 clarifies that, there should be no discrimination among any citizen (Kumar, 2013). As per Article 29(2), it has also been made clear that, no one shall be denied admission to educational institute maintained by the state. All these efforts were done to make inclusive education available to all the students without any discrimination or biasness. The success of inclusive learning schools largely depends on the school teachers, who are instrumental in creating inclusive classrooms.

History of Inclusive Education in India

India has always been considered a land of culture and education. From Vedic period, the education has been provided by Gurukuls and Rishikuls where students used to live with their teachers and learn by practical study and debates. There was no such special education provided to the students with disabilities; however, Patanjali was one to provide Yoga therapy to disabled persons. Later during Maurya Dynasty, it was strictly prohibited to abuse both verbally or behaviourally to people with disability. Later, King Ashoka established hospitals and asylums for treating disabled people. After that, Vishnu Sharma developed 'The Panchatantra', a legend to use animal fables for teaching children in an easy and entertaining way. Then comes the Mughal Empire which made a great progress in education followed by British East India Company with English and Convent education in the country. At the end of the second world war, Sir John Sargent, an educational advisor to the Government of India, prepared a Sargent Report in 1944. He recommended that there should be a provision for people with handicaps and they should be sent to a school for special children (Sargent Report, 1944).

Policies and Legislative Framework

After Independence, education came under Ministry of Education, whereby the Government of India created several policies for providing special education to the children with special needs (Chatterjee, 2015). Also, in 1964 the visionary Kothari Commission did recommend the inclusion of all children with disabilities in mainstream schools in their plan of Action (Gupta, 1984; Jangira, 1995; Julka, 2005). However, after independence in 1947, many acts have been passed by the Central Government to facilitate education to all the children in the past few years, but it was difficult to cross the attitudinal barriers to inclusive education. In 1953, the Central Social Welfare Board was created. Between 1960 and 1975 several committees were appointed to recommend a national policy which must focus especially on the needs of children of low socio-economic areas. It resulted in the formulation of the National Policy for Children in 1974 as also the National Children's Board. The major achievement was however the launch of the The Integrated Child Development Programme (ICDS) also in 1974, as a part of India's Fifth five-year plan. This is an excellent concept but the prime initial objectives were the decrease in infant mortality and training women in health care and nutrition. It broadened its scope only in 1975 to include a psychosocial component on non-formal early childhood education but as just one of the totals of six components it was designed to support. The District Primary Education Programme (DPEP), which followed focused on integration in the areas of teacher training, removing architectural barriers and in providing appropriate aids and did fare better but was unable to include a vast majority of children with disabilities in mainstream education (Pandey & Advani, 1995). The Government recognized that, people with disabilities also had the right to education as other citizens but the necessities of the nation which is grappling with problems like poverty, illiteracy, unemployment, malnutrition, and sheer survival needs of its people made it difficult to sustain focus on the development of services for disabilities. Thus, in 1986, the Parliament of India adopted the National Policy on Education (NPE) in which for the first-time equality of opportunity was formally stated as a goal of education and the phrase "education for the handicapped" was used. Although, the same policy was initiated earlier in 1968 and reformulated in 1985 but this time it focused only on the integration of children with locomotor disabilities and others with mild disabilities in mainstream schools. A team of experts was set under the chairmanship of Behrul Islam in 1987 to study the problems and challenges of disabled children which resulted in developing the Persons with Disabilities Act of 1995. The Act stresses the need to provide free of cost education to all children in an appropriate environment till they are 18 years old. It further emphasizes on the right of the disabled on the following measures:

a) Transport facilities to the students with disabilities or alternative financial incentives to parents or guardians to enable their students with disabilities to attend schools;
b) The removal of architectural barriers from schools, colleges or other institutions imparting vocational and professional training.
c) The supply of books, uniforms and other materials to students with disabilities attending school.
d) The grant of scholarship to students with disabilities.
e) Suitable modification in the examination system to eliminate purely mathematical questions for the benefit of blind students and students with low vision.
f) Restructuring of curriculum for the benefit of students with disabilities.
g) Restructuring the curriculum for benefit of students with hearing impairment to facilitate them to take only one language as part of their curriculum.

The National Trust Act (National Trust for the Welfare of Persons with Autism, Cerebral Palsy, Mental Retardation and Multiple Disability), 1999 also came into existence. This landmark legislation seeks to protect and promote the rights of persons who within the disability sector, have been even more marginalized than others. It was first of its kind in the category of persons addressed. The Salamanca Statement and Framework for Action on Special Needs Education (1994) emerged as a result of deliberations held by more than 300 participants present. The Ministry of Human Resource Development (MHRD) Action Plan MHRD has developed an action plan to spread the education to all the masses of society irrespective of their age, gender, or any socio-economic status. It was focused on catering to the needs and requirements of children with disability to enable them learn and be literate. An outline of MHRD action plan for disabled children has been presented below:

- To complement and supplement IEDC and Sarva Shiksha Abhiyan programmes in the movement from integration to inclusion.
- To enroll and retain children with disabilities in the mainstream education system.
- To provide need based educational and other support in mainstream schools to children in order to develop their learning and abilities, through

appropriate curricula, organizational arrangements, teaching strategies, resource and partnership with their communities.

- To support higher and vocational education through proper implementation of the existing reservation quota in all educational institutions and creation of barrier-free learning environments.
- To enable disability focused research and interventions in universities and higher educational institutions.
- To review the implementation of existing programmes, provisions to identify factors leading to success or failure of the drive towards enrollment and retention of children with disabilities in mainstream educational settings.
- To generate the awareness in the general community, activists and persons working in the field of education and more specifically among parents and children that the disabled have full rights to appropriate education in mainstream schools and that it is the duty of those involved in administration at every level including schools.
- To ensure the enrollment and intervention for all have access to education. Children with special needs in the age group 0-6 years in Early Childhood Care and Education Programmes.
- To facilitate free and compulsory elementary education for children with special needs in the age group 6-14 (extendable to 18 years.) in mainstream education settings currently under the Sarva Shiksha Abhiyan (SSA).
- To facilitate for transition of young persons with disability wishing to pursue secondary education.
- To ensure physical access of children and youth with disabilities in schools and educational institutions by enforcing the requirement for provisions of universal design in buildings and provide support in transportation.
- To develop national norms for inclusive education, to set standards of implementation, training, monitoring and evaluation for the programme.
- To provide inputs in all pre-service and in-service training for mainstream and special education teachers to enable them to work with children with disability in an inclusive education system.
- To provide appropriate resource services support through appointment of special educators, rehab professionals, provision of resource rooms, etc. to support mainstream school teachers in the classrooms.
- To put in place an effective communication and delivery system for specific delivery of TLM, aids and appliances, hardware/software.
- To participate in sports, co-curricular activities, and to promote all-round ability development.
- To ensure the physical access for young persons with disabilities (18 plus age group) in all colleges and higher educational institutions by enforcing the requirement for provisions of universal design in buildings and provide support in transportation.

But, in spite of having such strong theoretical and legislative framework in our country, the desired goal has not been achieved so far. This clearly points out to certain challenges that need immediate addressal if inclusive education for CWSN is to become a successful system. Research evidence shows that general school teachers' attitude towards education of children with special needs is not always positive and supportive. Most mainstream teachers do not believe that they have the skills and knowledge to do this kind of work and there is a need of special 'experts' to deal with such students on one-to-one basis.

Challenges to Inclusive Education

There are certain challenges to Inclusive Education which need immediate addressal because of the initiatives of the government to facilitate the inclusive education for the children with special needs. There has been considerable improvement in the enrolment of CWSN in the schools during last decade. This wide scale inclusion has challenged general teachers to change their perceptions of children with disabilities, their expectations and their roles in an inclusive classroom, as they will have to teach increasingly diverse students. This has put the teachers under pressure and faced many challenges, some of them are discussed below:

Poor Infrastructure: Most of the schools in rural villages lack proper infrastructural facilities and in some schools even the students are made to sit on the floor due to non-availability of furniture. Majority of the government schools lack basic facilities like proper toilets, playgrounds, libraries, safe drinking water, electricity etc. Although the government through SSA, RMSA, etc. has been trying to overcome these shortcomings by constructing buildings and toilets, yet there are many limitations that need to be properly addressed.

Ineffective Teaching Strategies: As teachers feel unprepared to teach CWSN and such huge diversity, their claim and excuse is that they do not have requisite knowledge, skills and suitable strategies to deal effectively with children with severe disabilities and specific needs. They need to be given orientation and training about suitable teaching skills.

Lack of Proper Awareness: There is a lack of proper awareness among parents, community members regarding the rights and provisions for the education of CWSN. Proper awareness will help in developing positive attitude and beliefs among them.

Financial Constraints: Due to liberalization and privatization, most of the schools and private institutes charge a very high fees or donation and it becomes impossible for people below poverty line to get their kids educated.

Conclusion

Inclusive education as strategy for facilitating inclusion rejects the idea of segregated education. There are many well defined policies, provisions and legislations that support and facilitate the education of CWSN. A lot has been achieved yet more needs to be done in terms of execution of these policies. The challenges need to be addressed to make inclusive education more effective. Keeping in view the limited resources and huge number of children who are still out of the ambit of education, inclusive education is the only way out to provide equitable education to all in terms of access and quality and non-discriminatory ways, which the entire world has been advocating and striving since so long.

References

Das, A.K., Kuyini A.B., & Desai I. P. (2013). Inclusive Education in India: Are the Teachers Prepared? *International Journal of Special Education*, 28(1), 27-36.

Singha Roy, D.K. (2014). *Towards a Knowledge Society: New Identities in Emerging India*. Cambridge University Press: New Delhi.

7

Inclusive Education
Challenges and Strategies

Satinder Kaur (Dr.)*

Introduction

The National Education Policy 2020 has conveyed the structural change in the education system which aims to make India the global knowledge superpower ensuring equity and inclusion. Materialisation of right to education is the pressing issue of our time. Education is the key to form tomorrow's productive citizens. It is not only a right but an enabler of all other rights. As the cornerstone of all educational decisions, the ray of hope has come through the National Education Policy 2020, which talks about sustainable human development and universal education-learning with equity and learning outcomes with research-oriented mindset. India has always placed education at the centre of its development agenda and with bridging the gender, social, regional gaps with community participation, it will raise the spirits towards equal opportunities to all ensuring equity in this policy. It is going to be a beautiful blend of both ancient and modern knowledge systems which not only inculcate you to acquire knowledge but also help in integrating Indian culture and ethos.

When the Western education system developed, it was to cater to mass education and disability was thought of to be an impairment that should be given special treatment in a separate environment. Since the medical profession was the one responsible for diagnosing the defects, it irrevocably became tied to it. It also became a screening process to keep the children with physical and sensory disabilities, and later also those with behavioural and learning disabilities, out of the mainstream school. However, the notion of Special Education was not very successful. Special segregated education has been the main vehicle for educating disabled children throughout most of the industrialised world in the twentieth century. Over a hundred years, a Special Education system has failed to provide disabled children with the knowledge and skills to take their rightful place in the world, and it has failed to empower them. However, a significant shift has been observed from Special Education to the Inclusive Education all over the world. The integration of disabled

*Assistant Professor, Dev Samaj College, Chandigarh

learners into mainstream schools has become an alternative to the presence of special schools, especially in the West.

Inclusive Education

It was the idea of Inclusive Education that radically altered the basis of Special Education and everything that it stood for, namely the growth of categories of disability and their subsequent rectification, the separation of education and the certification of teachers. The distinction between mainstream and inclusion is that while the former means the selective placement of Special Education students in one or more 'regular education classes' to the extent that these students can keep up with the work assigned by the teacher in the regular classroom while utilising the relevant educational services, inclusion means to structure the educational environment in such a way that it becomes possible to include students with special needs in the classroom itself. In other words, mainstream tries to bring children with special needs to fit them in the existing classroom methods and goals; inclusion approach tries to provide education that is responsive to the needs of all students. Inclusion tries to bring together the efforts of the general and the special educator to the child rather than the child moving for this support. The idea of inclusion is not a new one and it has its roots in liberal and progressive thought. The current schooling system seems to be based on two opposing avenues, that of integration and segregation. There were many like Elizabeth Burgwin, a child welfare pioneer, who saw no point in segregation and while thinking about the needs of disabled children, assumed that the adaptation that had to be made would be to the normal school. The other body of opinion dealt with the view that children could be divided according to the difficulties they faced and consequently special schools could be set up to cater to their needs. Instead of referring to children as having 'special needs', Inclusive Education sees these 'needs' as a part of diversity among learners who need equal treatment. While the emphasis when discussing about inclusion tends to emphasise on the curriculum, the attitudes and the teaching method, there is a further dimension which is related to inclusion not just in the classroom but in the overall society as well. Inclusion in most circumstances is understood as being opposed to the concept of segregation in a very similar way to which integration is seen as opposed to segregation. However, it is important to keep in mind that inclusion and integration are not synonyms. The word inclusion should be understood in opposition to exclusion. Integration thus focuses on the child and how the child should adapt to fit into the school whereas inclusion focuses on the school itself where it is the school which has to make adjustments to make the child fit in.

The Kothari Commission (1964-66) brought up the issue of education of children with special needs and was one of the first education commissions to do so. It recommended that — 'children with special needs should be integrated into ordinary schools. The education of such children should not be organized merely on the grounds of humanitarianism and pity but rather it should be such that education enables the individual overcome his/her handicap and emerge as a useful citizen of the country.' For this, the commission recommended that the Ministry of Education allot the necessary funds to help educated children with special needs. However, despite the recommendations of the commission, the needs of the children with special needs was relegated to the voluntary sector, where the government would give out funds for their welfare and thus maintain direct link the children.

Challenges of Inclusive Education

For Inclusive Education to be meaningful, schools must recognise and respond to the diverse needs of their students, accommodating both different styles and rates of learning and ensuring quality education to all through appropriate curricula, organisational arrangements, teaching strategies, resource use and partnership with their communities (UNESCO 1994). Teachers do not have support they need to make Inclusive Education successful. Inadequate financial provision remains one of the major obstacles in the implementation of meaningful programmes. Teachers training programme, adapted curriculum, teachers' attitude, materials and equipment's provision and financial sources are the major challenges in the implementation of Inclusive Education.

- *Problems for Classroom Teachers:* A classroom teacher is expected to select educational methodology to best suit each student. This is a challenging goal for a teacher who potentially has more than 30 students in each of five to seven classes. Most students can be grouped with other students whose educational needs are similar. This may reduce the planning required to two or three groups. If special needs students who have severe learning delays, developmental issues, or who speak little or no English are added, this task can become almost insurmountable especially if the inclusive classroom does not include a co-teacher.
- *Problems for Special Education Teacher:* The biggest problem for special education teachers who have students in inclusive classrooms is being available to every student. Students may have to be pulled out of class a few times a week for additional services, which also impacts the ability of the child and classroom teacher to maintain pace.
- *Problems for Students:* In a classroom of 30 students with one or two special education students, it can be difficult for the classroom teacher to give the individual time and attention the student requires and deserves.
- *Expenses:* Funding is a major constraint to the practice of inclusion. Teaching students with disabilities in general education classrooms takes specialists and additional staff to support students' needs. Financial difficulty is another barrier to Inclusive Education; lots of funds are required for physical infrastructure, teaching programme and further provision of jobs for disabled.

- *Lack of Trained Teachers:* Inclusive system needs trained teachers who can handle the persons with disabilities in normal classroom; but teachers are taught about special education and not about Inclusive Education.
- *Cooperation:* One of the barriers associated with Inclusive Education is a lack of communication among administrators, teachers, specialists, staff, parents, and students. Open communication and coordinated planning between general education teachers and special education staff is essential for inclusion to work. Time is needed for teachers and specialists to meet and create well-constructed plans to identify and implement modifications and accommodations and specific goals for individual students.

Teaching Strategies for Inclusive Education

Inclusive Education is a challenge for the teacher. The teacher must ensure maximum learning for all and equal opportunities for all. The teacher must ensure the participation of each student. Another one is peer tutoring. Sometimes a child learns better when taught by peers. Multisensory teaching allows the maximum use of senses for learning.

- ***Team Teaching:*** Team teaching is an approach in which two or more teachers join together, plan together, teach together and evaluate together. Inclusive schools, the regular education teacher and special education teacher work together in providing services to disabled children. It is the joint responsibility of both the teachers.
- ***Peer Tutoring:*** Peer tutoring involves one-to-one instruction from a student to another in the tutoring role and the tutee who receives instruction. Peer tutoring meets the individual needs of the child with disabilities by providing remedial or supportive instruction.
- ***Cooperative Learning:*** It is a strategy used by teachers in which they make groups of students to achieve a common goal.
- ***Language Experience Approach:*** This approach integrates the development of reading skills with the development of listening, speaking and writing skills.
- ***Multisensory Approach:*** Multisensory approach is based on the premise that for some children learning is facilitated if the content is presented through several modes.
- ***Breakthrough to Literacy Programme:*** This is a programme in which if a child cannot retain the material through reading, s/he can write it to retain it.
- ***Task Analysis:*** Through task analysis strategy the child learns the material by breaking up into small components. The components are broken, sequenced and transacted by the teacher to the child.
- ***Modifying Materials and Activities:*** Various other activities like discussions demonstrations, simulation, role-playing, and dramatic improvisation activities are used by the teacher in the classroom.

- ***Word Analysis Skills:*** Word analysis can be done through synthetic method and analytic method. Phonetic analysis teaches a student to attack an unfamiliar word.
- ***Assistive Technology:*** Teachers can create an effective environment in the classroom by using technology. Various types of Assistive Technologies are now available to students with disabilities. Assistive technology is technology used by individuals with difficulties in order to perform functions that might otherwise be difficult or impossible.

Reforms in Curriculum

Traditional curriculum cannot help Inclusive Education. It is necessary to bring the required changes in curriculum. Multilevel and flexible curriculum, cooperative curriculum, providing reading material, simple curriculum, participation in games, use of teaching aids adequate facilities are some of the areas where we need to work. National Curriculum Framework 2005 also focused on the reforms in curriculum for Inclusive Education. It stresses on the need to explore the abilities of children. Innovative and special strategies can be devised and used by teachers. Teaching-learning processes must be based on planning so that the needs of all children can be fulfilled. Children often learn language easily through special interaction. Braille and sign language can be used for special children. The school must have adequate playground, resource room etc. Activities must be planned, selected and executed in such a manner that individual attention is provided to each child.

Inclusive Classroom

Students with special needs are educated in regular classes for nearly all of the day, or at least for more than half of the day. Whenever possible the students receive any additional help or special instruction in the general classroom.

References

Government of India (1986). *National Policy on Education*, Ministry of Education: New Delhi.

Government of India (1992) *The Programme on Action 1992 of National Policy on Education 1986,* Ministry of Education: New Delhi.

Government of India (2012). *Report to the people on Education 2011-12* MHRD: New Delhi.

Government of India (2011). *All India Survey on Higher Education*, MHRD.

Planning Commission (2007). *The Eleventh Five Year Plan 2007-2012* Vol. I, II & III, Government of India: New Delhi.

Planning Commission (2013). *Twelfth Five Year Plan* 2012-17 Vol I, II & III. Government of India: New Delhi.

Singha Roy, D.K. (2014). *Towards a Knowledge Society: New Identities in Emerging India.* Cambridge University Press: New Delhi.

8

Enhancing Educational Opportunities for Differently Abled Students through Inclusive Education

Vibha Chawla (Dr.)*

Introduction

India is a country with many unique characteristics. Covering an area of 3.3 million square kilometers, India accounts for just 2.4% of the world's land area but contains over 16% of the total world's population, or one billion people. India's population comprises different ethnic, cultural, tribal and racial groups. With more than 1,500 dialects, 18 official languages and several religious communities — India is a country with rich diversity. The Constitution provides for uniform citizenship for the whole nation and ensures the Fundamental Rights of every Indian citizen, including freedom of speech, expression, belief, association, migration, choice of occupation irrespective of caste, creed, region and religion.

India has a rich history of education, at the time of its Independence, India inherited an educational system which was not only quantitatively small but was also characterised by regional, gender, caste and structural imbalances. The National Policy on Education 1986, and Program of Action 1992 both confirmed the government's commitment to improve the literacy levels in the country.

But if we talk about the ancient system of education (*guru-shishya parampara*), all children were taught together, be it under a shady tree or in the Gurukul (school): all children — normal, gifted, disabled either physically or intellectually — were considered as the beneficiaries of education according to their abilities to have education. In its true sense it was Inclusive Education.

India has a rich cultural inheritance for inclusive education. India was yesterday, today and in future will always be an inclusive society in the way that a very wide variety of cultural and religious beliefs exist side by side. Even

*Assistant Professor, Rayat-Bahra College of Education, Hoshiarpur

today, small rural schools provide education for all children under one roof, little realising that they are following a system of education newly rediscovered in the West termed as Inclusive Education. Two basic approaches to equalising educational opportunity dominated in the 20th century:

- Differentiation — matches to students' individual need;
- Universalism — standardises schooling meets the needs of all students collectively (Reeves, 2004).

Inclusive education is a way to achieve the aim of equalisation (means all the students have the same right to access education) of educational opportunities. Inclusive education is one of the better alternatives of providing education to children with disabilities in India (Shah et al., 2016).

Inclusive Instructional Practices

The rationale for inclusion has three main aspects:

- The ethical and human rights;
- Educational and social benefits to all learners;
- The legal requirement to include all children.

Inclusion is about ensuring that the rights of all children are met, that they can actively engage in education within their community. The student with additional needs is welcomed as a valued member within the setting. The inclusive instructional practices embrace all type of students disabled or non-disabled but there are a number of factors in the system that may interfere in achieving the goal of inclusive education. They are the barriers which lead to inability of the system to accommodate diversity and lead to learning breakdown.

Types of Barriers

- *Attitudinal Barrier:* Negative attitude and misbeliefs about the disabled.
- *Physical and environmental Barrier:* Difficulty for the disabled to reach at the desired place of learning.
- *Learning Experience Barriers:* Needed adoptions and modifications according to the learning needs of disabled are not made.
- *Barrier related to lack of resources and support:* Ill-prepared schools, poor infrastructure and scarcity of man material resources are harmful to the well-being of disabled.
- *Psychological Barriers:* Problems and difficulties faced by disabled with the abled students.
- *Barrier related to Educational policy:* Educational policies are framed according to the needs of a normal child and not according to the disabled.

Strategies to be Adopted

For ensuring equal access to educational opportunities for the full participation and development of all the learners, we must adopt inclusion in a quite sincere and effective way in our school system. The need of the hour is to work on two fronts:

First — to work for the removal of the existing barriers in the path of the learning and participation of disabled in inclusive school;
Second — to adopt such ways and means that can help in the creation of a conducive environment for the proper inclusion of the children with disabilities.

Paramount Points for Barrier-Free Inclusive Education

- Protect the disabled from distance barrier: admission of these students should be in the nearest regular school.
- Adequate transport facilities with needed disabled friendly.
- Disabled friendly environment and infrastructure for enabling proper access to the classroom and other workplace activities.
- Bring positive desirable changes in the attitude of the society, school authorities and teachers.
- Care should be taken that disabled children may not suffer from any unnecessary psychological set back.
- Parents, school authorities, people and disabled children themselves should be aware of the facilities available through programmes, policies and legislative measures.
- Maintenance of the flexibility in the curriculum and learning experience should be considered.
- Efforts should be made to modify pre-service and in-service teacher education programmes to equip the teacher with needed skills related to inclusive set up.
- Creation of a conducive environment for inclusion.
- Inclusion in the form of a full inclusion model should be accepted.
- Top priority should be for pre-service and in-service education in the classroom for equipping them with the necessary knowledge, skills, attitudes for working in an inclusive set up.
- Common instructional goals targeted in a normal non-inclusive set up should be established.
- The appropriate techniques and strategies, collaborative team approach, activity based learning, cooperative learning and experiences, data based instruction, creative problem solving, peer to peer supports practised by the teachers while working in the inclusive set up.

- Special education services in the form of resource room facilities, individualised guidance and help from the special teacher and professionals.

UNICEF'S Work to Promote Inclusive Education

UNICEF supports government efforts to foster and monitor inclusive education systems so that the education gap for children with disabilities can be reduced. UNICEF work focuses on four key areas:

- *Advocacy:* UNICEF promotes inclusive education in discussions, high-level events and other forms of outreach geared towards policymakers and the general public.
- *Awareness-raising:* UNICEF shines a spotlight on the needs of children with disabilities by conducting research and hosting roundtables, workshops and other events for government partners.
- *Capacity-building:* UNICEF builds the capacity of education systems in partner countries by training teachers, administrators and communities, and providing technical assistance to governments.
- *Implementation support:* UNICEF assists with monitoring and evaluation in partner countries to close the implementation gap between policy and practice.

There was a time when children with any exceptionality lying in them were thought as a matter of great concern. That time exceptional were forced to suffer from isolation from the mainstream society. Inclusive education is concerned with the education and accommodation of ALL children in society, regardless of their physical, intellectual, social, or linguistic deficits. Children from disadvantaged groups should also be included in Inclusion, of all races and cultures as well as the gifted and the disabled. Inclusion tries to reduce exclusion within the education system by taking every possible step either it is tackling, responding to and meeting the different needs of all learners (Booth, 1996). It involves changing the education system so that it can accommodate the unique styles and way of learning of each learner and ensure that there is quality education for all through the use of proper resources, suitable curricula, appropriate teaching strategies and partnerships within the community (UNESCO, 1994).

Inclusion and Inclusive Practices in Education

Inclusive education allows equal opportunity for students with a disability to enter mainstream schools with students without a disability. Inclusion is the right of a child and parents to participate in mainstream schools or in special schools, and acceptance of the child and to adjust him in the best way possible is the responsibility of the school. Every child has a right to achieve his goals along with satisfaction and self-achievement. There is need to focus on social inclusion, to improve positive outcomes for disadvantage students in mainstream schools. The social inclusion initiative acknowledges the groups that fall into the category of most disadvantaged groups or individuals. The aim is to improve outcomes for these people or groups.

Techniques for Inclusive Classrooms

Students in an inclusive classroom are generally placed with their chronological age-mates and to encourage a feeling of belonging, emphasis is placed on the value of friendships. The present skill levels of regular school teachers needs to be improved for teaching students with disabilities in inclusive education setup (Das et al., 2013). Teachers often nurture a relationship between a student with special needs and a same-age student without a special educational need.

To build common classroom communities different techniques are used by the teachers:

- Using games
- Involving students in problem solving
- Sharing songs and books
- Dealing with individual differences by adopting different strategies
- Assigning classroom jobs
- Teaching students to look for ways to help each other
- Encouraging students to take the role of teacher and deliver instruction (e.g. read a portion of a book to a student with severe disabilities)
- Focusing on the strength of a student with special needs
- Create classroom checklists
- Take breaks when necessary
- Create an area for children to calm down
- Organise student desk in groups
- Create a self and welcoming environment
- Set ground rules and stick with them
- Help establish short-term goals
- Design a multi-faced curriculum
- Communicate regularly with parents and/or caregivers
- Seek support from other special education teachers.

Teaching Models for Inclusionary Practices

The teachers must be adequately trained at pre-service level to teach in inclusive teaching setup so as to effectively teach all students in inclusive, diverse and collaborative settings (Whitworth, 1999). The designing and building appropriate teaching model for practices to demonstrate to prospective teachers for their success in the inclusive teaching environment. Some of the models for inclusive teaching practices are:

- One teach, one support: In this model, the content teacher will deliver the lesson and the special education teacher will assist students' individual needs and enforce classroom management as needed.
- One teach, one observe: In this model, the most experienced teacher will deliver the lesson and the other teacher will float or observe.
- Station teaching (rotational teaching): In this model, the room is divided into parts in which the students will visit with their small groups. Generally, the content teacher will deliver the lesson in his/her group, and the special education teacher will complete the adapted version of the lesson with the students.
- Parallel teaching: In this model, one half of the class is taught by the content teacher and one half is taught by the special education teacher. Both groups are being taught the same lesson, just in a smaller group.
- Alternative teaching: In this method, the content teacher will teach the lesson to the class, while the special education teacher will teach a small group of students an alternative lesson.
- Team teaching (content/support shared 50/50): Both teachers share the planning, teaching and supporting equally. This is the traditional method, and often the most successful.

Policy and Procedures

The National Policy for Persons with Disability, 2006 clearly delineates the framework under which the state, civil society and private sector must work for upliftment of persons with disability. The Right of Children for Free and Compulsory Education, 2009 assures free and compulsory education to all children. The Government of India has launched a number of schemes to promote Inclusive Education. The education policy in India showed increased focus on children and adults with special needs (Singh, 2016). Rights of Persons with Disabilities Act, 2016 includes a number of provisions for inclusive education (Kumar & Kumar, 2018).

Conclusion

It must be ensured that educators providing inclusive education have undergone special training so that they can give their best in the inclusive teaching environment. The teachers should have adequate resources to teach students with diverse needs and learning styles. The Government and Non-Government Organisations working in the area of inclusive education should provide suitable financial assistance to support all activities and services. The complete plan of inclusive education should be reframed by involving educators, social workers, parents and students. The barriers in inclusive education are to be removed by government making and implementing sound policies and legislation. All this will increase the movement of students from special schools to mainstream schools. This will not only result in efficient and effective use of investment made in mainstream schools but also enhance the educational opportunities for students with different abilities.

References

Booth, T. (1996). A perspective on inclusion from England. *Cambridge Journal of Education*, 26(1), 87–99.

Das, A.K., Kuyini A.B., & Desai I.P. (2013). Inclusive Education in India: Are the Teachers Prepared? *International Journal of Special Education*, 28(1), 27-36.

Kumar, S. & Kumar, S. (2018). RPwD ACT, 2016 and School Education: Concerns And Challenges. *International Journal of Research and Analytical Reviews*, 5(1), 382-385.

Ministry of Human Resource Development. *National Policy on Education (PoA-1992).* New Delhi: Government of India.

Reeves, J. (2004). "Like Everybody Else": Equalizing Educational Opportunity for English Language Learners. *TESOL Quarterly*, 38(1), 43-66.

Shah, R., Das, A.K., Desai, I.P. and Tiwari, A. (2016). Teachers concerns about inclusive education in Ahmedabad, India. *Journal of Research in Special Educational Need*, 16(1), 34-45.

Singh, J.D. (2016). Inclusive Education in India – Concept, Need and Challenges. *Scholarly Research Journal for Interdisciplinary Studies*, 3(16), 3919-3925.

UNESCO (1994). The Salamanca Statement and Framework for Action on Special Needs Education. World Conference on Special Needs Education: Access and Quality Salamanca, Spain, 7-10 June 1994. *https://www.european-agency.org/sites/default/files/salamanca-statement-and-framework.pdf.*

Whitworth, J.W. (1999). A Model for Inclusive Teacher Preparation, *Electronic Journal for Inclusive Education*, 1 (2), 1-11.

9

Inclusive Pedagogy for Inclusive School

Madhuri Isave (Dr.)*

Introduction

Inclusive education in National Education Policy 2020 seems to have given a lot of thought to the issue of inclusiveness in higher education. There is still a need to create awareness about inclusive education in India. It takes time to create a common framework. At present, inclusive education seems to be the most talked about concept. Inclusive education is a broad concept. Recent technological, social and cultural changes have added new challenges to education around the world, especially internationally. It is imperative that teachers use a universal design to ensure equal access to all students due to the inclusive concepts. In terms of pedagogy, the teaching methods mainly include teaching theory, classroom processing and evaluation, etc. In the process of teaching students, imparting information, adding new information, inculcating values and keeping all students on equal footing, is raising their level of knowledge.

Different approaches are expected to be used in inclusive teaching. Depending on the student's learning style and student behaviour, different programmes may be involved. In order to have effective interaction between teacher and student, some activities must be included. It is important to consider the elements of teaching in an inclusive teaching method. Art is the art of teaching. The teacher is an important factor in this. He has to master this art. In order to carry out this process properly, the teacher has to follow some essential principles. The environment, time limits, student progress, etc., and to do this, it is very important for the teacher to understand the different perspectives of pedagogy.

The different perspectives of pedagogy are behavioural constructivism, social constructivism, and logical thinking etc.

Pedagogical Philosophy of Flexible Learning

Pedagogical Philosophy of Flexible learning is learner-centred, encouraging greater independence and autonomy on the part of the learner. Its ethos is to

* Associate Professor, Tilak College of Education, Pune

enable and empower learners and give them greater control of their learning and become more self-directed. It increases choices available to both learners and teachers resulting in a 'blurring of traditional internal/external boundaries' (George & Luke, 1995).

Concept of flexibility also includes flexibility of admissions and enrolment processes, flexibility in assessment and assessment times. Introducing flexibility or increasing flexibility is not necessarily 'good' in itself. The key issue is how it impacts on student learning and the quality of that learning experience. It is about improving learning outcomes and maximising learner engagement using appropriate learning approaches.

There is no common definition of flexible education (Casey & Wilson, 2005; King & Kenworthy, 1999; Kirkpatrick & Jakupec, 1999; Nicoll, 1998). The following selected definitions are meant to convey an overview of the term.

'Flexible learning expands choice on what, when, where and how people learn. It supports different styles of learning, including e-learning' (DEST).

'A generic term that covers all those situations where learners have some say in how, where and when learning takes place – whether within the context of traditional institution centred courses or in non-traditional contexts such as open learning, distance learning, CAT schemes, wider-access courses or continuing professional development' (Ellington, 1997 p. 4).

'Flexible provision of higher education refers here to a mode of provision that provides learners with guided choice, in a number of domains, achieved through employment of various strategies including the use of learning and teaching techniques and technologies and the adoption of policies affecting choices for learners'.

('The Effectiveness of Models of Flexible Provision of Higher Education', 2001, DEST, Australian Government, Department of Education Employment and Workplace Relations, 2008).

Best Practices for Inclusive School

Service provider — While working with diverse learners, teacher has to play multiple roles as per the need of the learners. In such a school, a teacher has to provide service in the form of guidance, supporting help for the students. Service learning principle may adopt in inclusive school. Strengthen collaborative services in the school for making inclusive services more successful.

Use different teaching strategies —

- Mini group of diverse learners
- Create classroom centres
- Blend 'the Basics' with more specialised instruction
- Rotate learning
- Thematic instructional
- Diversification of books and materials.

Mini group: For better results make the group of 2 or 3 students within a class according to their levels and skills. The teaching and instructions can be separate for each group, e.g. in maths class one group could be working on basics while a more advanced group could be working on their geometry skills. Students would be grouped together according to similar skill levels and objectives along their education pathway.

Create classroom centres: Classroom centres are another effective way students can be grouped. Each centre would specialise in one area or level. The centres would be self-contained in terms of instructions and all lesson materials. They would also be somewhat self-explanatory and self-guided to allow the teacher to rotate among the different centres and provide appropriate guidance. A teaching assistant, parent or volunteer could help facilitate the groups. Such centres would strike a balance between being self-explanatory without totally giving up more direct teacher time.

Blend "the Basics" with more specialised instruction: Teacher can explain the general concepts to the whole group and then make the pairs for individual instruction. Since every school subject has some general concepts that could be relevant, individual students can benefit from this no matter what their level of proficiency. Reading comprehension strategies, the basics of maths organising, writing ideas or even a scientific theory are some examples of general concepts that could be taught to support what each student is learning in that area. Students can then apply this knowledge to their particular individual assignments. However the teacher could always add some additional content for more advanced students.

Rotate learning: Lessons within the different groups or centres could be rotated so that on any given day the teacher could introduce new material to one group while other groups only have to be checked who are doing more independent activities. The teacher assistant could also give service within such a lesson cycle.

Thematic instruction: Thematic instruction is where a single theme is tied into multiple subject areas. This method of teaching has been shown to be very effective in special education classrooms. A "theme" could be anything from a current event, having the skill of reading comprehension, a writing topic or historical event. For example, a historical event could be tied into all other subjects. The theme should be attention-getting-something that will grab the students' interest and keep them engaged.

Provide different levels of books and materials: Since there will be a variety of proficiency levels in the classroom, we can keep different levels of textbooks and other teaching materials available for each subject. If we keep a range of levels on hand it will ensure that each student can learn at the appropriate level. This will minimize frustration and maximize confidence and forward momentum in the student. No matter what the content areas of the variety of levels your students are working on, harmony and integration are possible.

All these teaching strategies are helpful to provide ideal instruction and support within their Inclusive classes.

Classroom Activities: The teacher can follow following classroom activities

- Instruction — Teacher gives instruction to the students to solve examples by guiding them. Maths slate and types of interaction was question-answers and individualised instructions.
- For visually impaired teachers can use Braille books in English with writing slates and braille books. Give Maths examples on Maths slates.
- Verbal instruction method used, audio headsets and CDs given to students
- Vocational skills taught like designing the lamps, painting the lamps by various colours.
- Body parts and their functioning activity
- A to Z alphabets practice
- Drawing, singing, making rakhis
- Alphabets, numerical maths, stories, poems, solving exercise books
- Demonstration, acting, modelling
- Displaying flashcards, asking questions, show charts as per lesson
- Asking the questions, display the cards, using flashcards
- Interaction depends on lesson
- Mostly with question answers, sign language,
- Lip matching
- Counting the various things (day-to-day objects like bottle, straw, money, feather
- Story telling as per the content, question-answer sessions.

Use of proper language — Teachers keep in mind themselves to use proper language for the students. Do not say the 'disabled person', say 'person with disability'. Say 'student with visually impairment' do not say 'blind student'. It is important while dealing with learners in the classroom.

A flipped classroom — A flipped classroom is an instructional strategy and a type of blended learning that reverses the traditional learning environment by delivering instructional content; often online outside of the classroom. It moves activities including those that may have traditionally been considered homework, into the classroom. In this approach instead of delivering lectures, material to study is given in the form of videos and students have to study and prepare the material at home. In the class they have to solve assignments in which the teacher would guide or help them to achieve their goals. It is observed by most of the teachers that it is the most beneficial to students. To apply the potential of flipped classrooms to special children and to think on how this flipped classroom approach would be useful to the children with special needs. Flipped classroom approach can be a useful and effective methodology for diverse learners. Flipped learning is a pedagogical approach in which the conventional notion of classroom-based learning is inverted so that students are introduced to the learning material before class, with classroom time then being used to deepen understanding through discussion with peers and problem solving facilitated.

Competent teacher — General teacher may not understand the concept of Inclusion. Does it mean education for person with disability only? Or need to concentrate only person with disability in classroom? Inclusive education ensures the participation of all students in schooling and acknowledge that all children can learn without any discrimination. Education cannot be considered quality education unless it meets the need of all learners. To understand the concept and meaning of inclusive education teacher has to accept diversity first and bring variety in teaching pedagogy as per learners' need and their learning style.

Present Status

In present scenario use of digital gadgets for teaching-learning is phenomenal, so the teachers' digital competency is important. In many rural regions/ remote areas there are established schools but with lack of equipment. Infrastructural facilities are not in good condition. Some schools have good infrastructure and sound technical devices but teachers have no competency to use the technology. We have to develop competency among teachers because only teacher can bring positive desirable change among students. We can suggest advanced pedagogy like service learning, self- directed learning as envisioned in NEP 2020.

In the current situation to identify strength, gap and areas for improvement in Inclusive education there is a need to develop understanding of Inclusive education. Need to change in evaluation and assessment procedure both in scholastic and non-scholastic areas of teaching-learning. We observed in inclusive schools there is no extra provision in curriculum design and assessment process

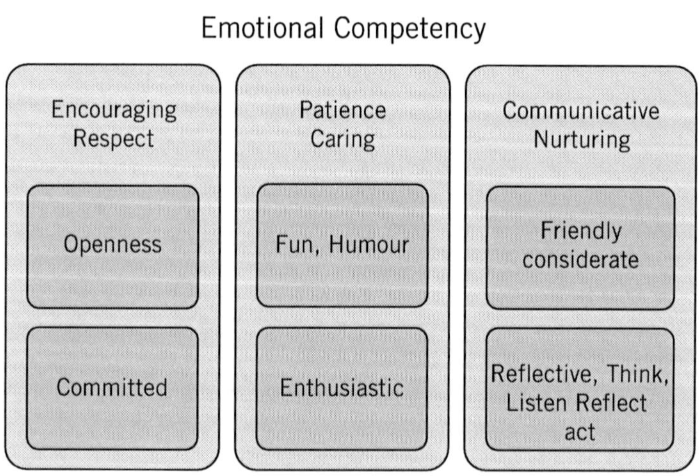

for disabled students. For example, in teacher training colleges the same curriculum and common evaluation strategy is implemented for all students. It is injustice for disabled students. So we need to change curriculum, content design and assessment to manage inclusive teaching and learning. School and inclusive education work efficiently when parents, community teachers come together and collect information about barriers in inclusive education, look at the causes and identify solutions.

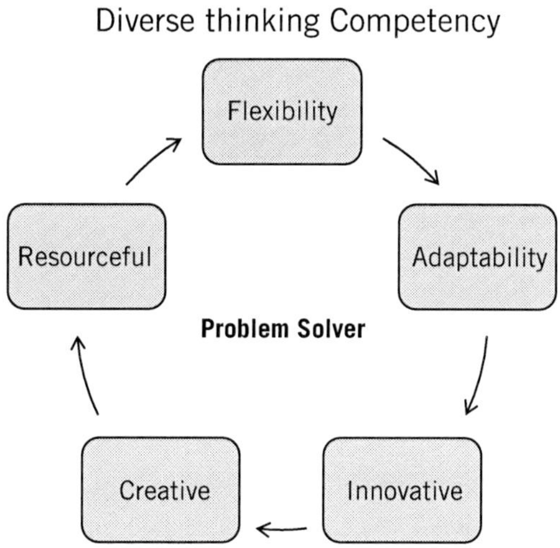

Conclusion

For successful inclusion and to make an effective inclusive school we need to train teachers. Focus on inclusive pedagogy so that every learner can take benefit for successful learning. Learner-centred pedagogy is promoted in inclusive schools and to make teachers aware about inclusive pedagogy it should be included in teacher training courses. More researchers have come up and taken research in inclusive education area. It is an urgent need to find research gap and a strategic plan should be prepared.

References

Ajuwon, P.M. 2008. Inclusive education for students with disabilities in Nigeria: benefits, challenges and policy implications. *International Journal of Special Education*, 23(3),11.

Beacham, N., & Rouse, M. (2012). Student teachers attitudes and beliefs about inclusion and inclusive practice. *Journal of Research in Special Educational Needs*. 12 (1), 3-11.

Lindsay, S., Proulx, M., Scott, H., & Thomson, N. (2014). Exploring teachers strategies for including children with autism spectrum disorder in mainstream classrooms. *International Journal of Inclusive Education*, 18(2), 101-122

https://www.afb.org

https://braillework.com

https://research.fb.com

https://www.henshaws.org

http://www.researchgate.net

10

Innovative Teaching Strategies for Inclusive Education

Pooja Sharma[*]

Introduction

Pedagogy is an art of sharing knowledge and information to the learners, which is dynamic in nature and the skill of dispersing of information may vary from teacher to teacher, classroom to classroom, institution to institution and platform to platform. The most critical factor in pedagogy is the constructivism. An effective pedagogical approach may touch upon the following:

- Pedagogies are consistently evolving processes; every pedagogy is different and may be modified as per 21st century learning scenarios.
- Pedagogy must fit the targeted audience i.e. learners and focus on helping students to develop an understanding of the knowledge delivered and relate with real life experiences.
- To enrich classroom experiences, various tools or methods may be integrated to enhance level of interaction and discussion within the class.
- Different assessment and evaluation tools need to be explored for higher and inclusive productivity of the learners. Integrating ICT into assessment and evaluation processes may provide self-assessment opportunity to learners.

Innovative Pedagogical Strategies

The adjectival word 'innovative' connotes new methods that are novel, advanced and original and in the context of innovative pedagogical strategies, it may be understood to be those pedagogical strategies which involve usage of appropriate means (tools) and methods (ways) in a new and creative ways and in their best combinations in order to make the teaching-learning process more effective and efficient by enabling the learners to attain the expected learning outcomes, develop students' capabilities in problem-solving, teamwork, learning to learn, reflective thinking etc. to be creative, adapt to changes, manage and analyze

[*]Assistant Professor, Khalsa College of Education, Amritsar

information, and work with knowledge. Innovative pedagogical approaches positively influence student learning, behaviour and attitudes and are capable of ensuring that all students achieve the defined course learning outcomes in specified period of time and demonstrate the expected learning outcomes. Para 13.4 of NEP 2020 recognizes flexibility for teachers to adopt innovative pedagogies to ensure a motivated and creative teacher.

Pedagogical Strategies Addressing Learning Needs

Pedagogy, as a focus for teaching and learning, involves reflecting on different pedagogical strategies and helping teachers to improve and innovate the art of teaching and learning. The changing environmental paradigms require new types of learners that bring creativity in the process of higher education by developing and cultivating conducive environment. Therefore, a teacher must assess and analyze students' learning needs to adopt the matching pedagogical approach. Further, different students' learning methods may vary. Some are fast in learning while reading texts and others ensure first listening to the teacher. Another group of students may learn once they have a practical demonstration. A teacher could find the ways to maintain the balance that will be favourable and conducive to every student. The learner's learning needs represent the gap between the learning experience one wants to have and their current state of knowledge, skill, and enthusiasm. There are four different domains of potential learning needs, viz., Cognitive, Social, Affective and Psychomotor, and these are detailed below in table:

Table 1: Domains of Learning Needs

Cognitive	*Social*	*Affective*	*Psychomotor*
Recognize good questions	Communicate with peers	Attain goals	Be in a comfortable setting
Ask good questions	Give and receive support	Nurture positive attitudes	Have transportation
Get help from experts	Experience external motivation	Be open to feedback from others	Have childcare
Practise problem-solving	Make a difference	Have time for reflection and self-assessment	Get enough sleep
Think independently	Interact while problem-solving	Possess well-founded self-confidence	Have a good diet/ adequate energy level
Create work products	Explore and challenge conventions	Define and respond to the locus of control	Exercise
Process new information	Grow with friends	Have a sense of belonging	Have access to equipment and tools

The diversity of learning needs of the learners occurs due to the nature of the discipline, course, level of study, necessary level of competency, and applicability of knowledge. Therefore, identification of specific learning needs of various learners is required to reflect in the learning outcomes of a course, which in turn are expected to reflect in the behaviour of the learners.

Innovative Teaching Strategies for Teaching in Inclusive Setting

Research has shown that Inclusive Education results in improved social development and academic outcomes for all learners. It leads to the development of social skills and better social interactions because learners are exposed to real environment in which they have to interact with other learners each one having unique characteristics, interests and abilities. The non-disabled peers adopt positive attitudes and actions towards learners with disabilities as a result of studying together in an inclusive classroom. Thus, inclusive education lays the foundation for an inclusive society accepting, respecting and celebrating diversity. This inclusive approach of including children with special needs in regular classrooms challenges teachers, schools, and districts to re-examine traditional beliefs and practices. In addition, new strategies must be developed to address the unique challenges of the inclusive education and ensure the success of both special and general education students. Multiple approaches to teaching-learning allow the teaching-learning process to keep pace with current and future developments. The following pedagogies emphasize constructive learning and active involvement of children with special needs in their learning journey, fulfilling the need of 21st Century learning environment:

- *Team Teaching:* Team teaching is an approach in which two or more teachers join together, plan together, teach together and evaluate together. As an educator, you have to work out the depth in which the therapists and doctors give their inputs and how they can be related to education and behaviour of the child in school. In inclusive schools, the regular education teacher and the special education teacher also work together in providing service to children with special needs in the classroom. In inclusive education, meeting the special educational needs of children is the joint responsibility of the regular teacher, the special teacher and other professionals. For team teaching, you have to plan jointly with others for teaching and evaluating a particular topic or subject depending upon your expertise/experience.
- *Peer Tutoring:* Peer tutoring involves one-to-one instruction from a student to another in the tutoring role and the tutee who receives instruction. Peer tutoring meets the individual's needs of the child with disabilities by providing remedial or supportive instruction. Following procedure is involved in peer tutoring:

- Make an assessment and evaluation of pupil's performance in the class.
- Prepare a comprehensive profile of tutee's performance in all areas of development.
- Recognise the strengths and weaknesses of the pupils in the class to select peer tutors.
- Match the tutor and the tutee. The tutor should be good in the subject and should have the skills to transact what the tutee with loco motor disability has to learn.
- Develop adapted instructional materials in advance for use by the peer tutor and tutee.
- Organize a short training programme for tutors for carrying out tutoring effectively for children with Special Need.
- Acknowledge the feedback to peer tutor about the present profile of the tutee and levels expected from the tutee in a particular time frame set for the child. Give very specific instructions to the peer tutor and to the tutee.
- Allot space and suitable work environment for tutoring.
- Keeping in mind the convenience of both, work out a practical work schedule.
- Reinforce the tutor for doing his job well and the tutee for the progress made by him.
- Build good relationships between them by encouraging both of them for their performance.
- Monitor the progress of tutoring.
- Change the tutor for different subjects or for different tests or for revision if the need be.

Above all, seek the permission from the tutor and the parents of the tutee for this activity. They have to be convinced that it is useful for both. Parents need to be told that the tutor also learns by teaching and the tutee learns better this way. Parents of the tutee need to be oriented to the disability and they need to be ensured that it will not affect their child in any adverse way.

- *Cooperative Learning*: Cooperative learning is a strategy used by group of students to achieve a common goal with mutual collaboration and support. In an inclusive classroom where a large number of children with and without disabilities have been enrolled, children can be taught with the help of cooperative learning in which they have common goals. If a child with special needs is to be taught he/she should be placed with the children who have the sensitivity and skills to deal with them. They need to be told about the difficulties the child faces and in what ways they can be of help. Grouping should be such that they help each other learn, they work together to seek solutions to problems and to complete an assignment. It is opposed to the existing system of education in the regular classroom where children are forced to compete against one another; the educational system encourages children to learn cooperatively through joint ventures. Using cooperative learning will provide opportunities to children with special needs, as they would take turns, ask questions, seek assistance, answer questions, offer suggestions, learn and display good manners, speak positively about others and correct others. The teacher would act only as a *Planner, Facilitator, Evaluator and Monitor.* The support material to carry out the task is also rotated. Conduct the activity in such a way that each child has to take responsibility for his own learning. Thus individual accountability is ensured. Cooperative learning is also used in a situation where a large number of children are on roll as in Municipal Corporation schools or rural schools in remote areas where we have one/two-teacher schools. It benefits not only children with special educational needs but also all other children. It promotes academic achievement, develops problem-solving skills, leadership skills and pro-social skills; increases motivation, understanding, retention and transfer of learning to varied situations. Thus, cooperative learning provides opportunities to all children to participate and contribute for the progress of the community.

- *Breakthrough to Literacy Programmed*: Many children cannot remember what they read as it seems very remote from their immediate environment. If they are taught to write what they are actually doing they should be able to retain it. Hence a strategy that could promote retention over a long period of time should be based on involvement of the child at different levels. One such strategy called 'Breakthrough To Literacy Programmed' could be used with children having special needs, as some children with hearing impairment, mental retardation cerebral palsy and spinal bifida may not be able to read easily. The strategy involves following steps:
    - The child narrates his experiences
    - The cards consisting of letters and words spoken are prepared
    - The teacher arranges the cards as child narrates
    - The teacher reads its out
    - The child repeats it till the children can read it independently.
- *Task Analyses*: In task analysis, the task to be learnt by the child is broken up into small teachable components. The components are sequenced and each component is transacted to the child. The next component to be taught is taken up only after the child masters the initial ones. Children with special needs cover a large range of disabilities. For each child the basal level and the profile have to be assessed and accordingly considering his

pace of learning, the task is to be broken down. Various activities of daily living as need academic activities can be taught through this method.

- *Modifying Materials and Activities*: Within the classroom teachers can employ discussions, demonstrations, and learning centres. Other intriguing techniques involve simulation activities, role-playing, or dramatization. Some additional techniques that teachers can utilize to enhance student performance in inclusive classroom settings are presented according to instructional methodology like field trips to museums, historical sites, and community locations can be engaged.
- *Critical Pedagogical Approach*: This approach emphasizes enhancing the learners' critical thinking skills by raising questions such as what they are learning and why they are learning, problem posing, and letting the students discover the answers. Learners acquire knowledge by investigation.
- *Game-Based Teaching*: Game-based teaching methods help students enjoy and not feel bored during teaching lessons. It allows students to be better engaged and not feel stressed. Students who are not quite good at studying can find this way of teaching helpful in learning and memorizing. Teachers need to ensure that students access the same type of data for game-based teaching. Teachers start teaching using video conferencing tools, including gaming sessions and may chat through the chat option with students asking questions.
- *Group discussions*: The use of discussions is an attempt to counteract the risk of the teacher taking a transmissive or authoritarian approach, enabling the learner group to explore their own and others views. In an inclusive classroom setting, group discussions encourage active listening, self-reflection, and the exchange of different cultural narratives, worldviews and attitudes of the students with diverse needs.

Conclusion

In a nutshell, inclusive education refers to an approach, seeks to address the learning needs of all children youth and adults with a specific focus on those who are vulnerable to marginalization and exclusion. Therefore, innovative teaching strategies help to modify the learning environment according to the diverse needs of the learners and make the teaching-learning environment more joyful and interesting. It implies all learners, young people — with or without disabilities being able to learn together through access to common pre-school provisions, schools and community educational setting with an appropriate network of support services. This is possible only in a flexible education system that assimilates the needs of a diverse range of learners and adapts itself to meet these needs. It aims at all stakeholders in the system (learners, parents, and community, teachers, and administrators, policy makers) to be comfortable with diversity and see it as a challenge rather than a problem.

References

Chaudhary, Aanyaa and Singh, Raghuvir (2018). *Research as a pedagogical tool in Higher Education Programmes:* Research Gate.

Delivery Types – Be safe Training Ltd. https://besafetraining.co.nz/delivery-types/ Education for Sustainable Development (ESD). https://1library.net/article/education-for- sustainable-development-esd.q595w1rz

Gupta, B.L., and Choubey, A. K. (2021). Higher Education Institutions–Some Guidelines for Obtaining and Sustaining Autonomy in the Context of NEP 2020. *Higher Education, 9(1).*

Government of India Ministry of Education Department of Higher Education (2022). Draft National Higher Education Qualifications Framework. Retrieved from https://www.ugc.ac.in. Med, C. I. (2006). Multidisciplinary, interdisciplinary and trans-disciplinarily in health research, services, education and policy: 1. Definitions, objectives, and evidence of effectiveness. Clin Invest Med, 29(6), 351-364.

Draft University Grants Commission (Minimum Standards and Procedures for Award of Ph.D. Degree) Regulations, 2022. Available: https://www.ugc.ac.in/pdfnews/4405511_Draft- UGC-PhD-regulations-2022.pdf

National Council of Educational Research and Training (2005), National Curriculum Framework. http://nceret.nic.in/pdf/nc-framework/nf2005-english.pdf

Sharma, K. (2002). *Self-Learning Material for Teacher Educators: Education of Children With Locomotor disabilities.* Department of Education of Groups with Special Needs, National Council of Educational Research and Training, Sri Aurobindo Marg, New Delhi-110016

United Nations Educational, Scientific and Cultural Organization. (2011). Education for Sustainable Development.

11

Inclusive Education in India
Issues, Challenges and Prospects

Anju Sharma* and Pallavi Sharma**

Introduction

There are many reasons for the success of teaching process. One of these is inclusion. Inclusion is one of the most widely studied topics in the teaching and learning process in the educational fields. A lot of researches have been done about its importance, its effect and the way it is applied. The Chinese proverb (IRC, 2006) says, "Tell me and I forget, teach me and I remember, involve me and I learn." The classroom is built upon interaction, cooperation, group work, and participation. These can be done through inclusion. If there is exclusion, teaching process would not be successful. Inclusion is one of the elements which, if applied properly, school achieves success. Inclusion lexically means the act of including or the state of being included. Therefore, Hudson (2009) explained that successful teachers should include their students as well as make their students included. Inclusion is about equal opportunities for all pupils. Pupils should all be included regardless of their age, gender, ethnicity, attainment and background. It gives attention and concentration to all pupils. In my opinion, successful inclusion is a must inside the classroom. When pupils are included properly, they will equally have the same chance to achieve, learn and acquire new experiences inside their school. But exclusion means bias, failure and drawback. Pupils should be taught, assessed, evaluated and supported equally. But teachers should consider that some pupils need more support or provision to have an equal chance of success. Inclusion needs planning and teaching inclusively. Therefore, each unit gives supported tasks to reach inclusion inside classrooms. To achieve a high rate of inclusion, teachers should put no limit for pupils' involvement. Broadly, inclusion not only means to include pupils inside their classrooms, but it also means to include classrooms inside their schools (Hudson 2009).

---

* Assistant Professor, Khalsa College of Education, Amritsar

** B.Ed.M.Ed. student, Khalsa College of Education, Amritsar

Issues and Challenges

The process of removing obstacles from learning and participation for all children and adolescents can also be considered. According to a Ministry of Education rule, "Inclusive education is an educational system that provides for all pupils," all learners should have the chance to work together in this setting. It should be encouraged for bright and talented children with special needs to attend regular schools and take part in extra-curricular activities separate from those offered to typical students. However, there are still some problems and difficulties that make achieving the goals difficult. These are as follows:

- *Absence of Supportive Equipment:* In inclusive classrooms, there are not enough assistive devices to help special children get the most out of their classes.
- *Greater Power Point usage Classroom Presentations:* Nowadays, we use technologies to create our teaching and learning processes more successful, but when we have a diverse group of students in the same class, we overlook the needs of special pupils.
- *Lower Student Enrollment:* In the mainstream school system, the enrolment rate of children with disabilities is to be at least on level with that of non-disabled students.
- *Incapacity of teachers:* Teachers are the most important factor in ensuring that inclusive education is implemented successfully. Teachers lack the competence, knowledge, and educational qualities that are expected of them in order to achieve the specified goal.
- *Massive class size:* The ability of special pupils to fully participate in normal classes is affected by large class size.
- *Teaching Techniques:* In most institutions, just a few predetermined teaching methods are used, resulting in differently abled pupils being unable to fully benefit from the teaching-learning process.
- *An absence of community interaction and will:* There appears to be a lack of parental and community willingness to send their children to mainstream institutions.
- *Unwillingness of the Political Class to Implement Inclusive Education:* Lack of political will to implement inclusive education is one of the most significant obstacles to putting the inclusive dream into practice.
- *Retention of Children with Disabilities in Schools:* Unavailability of peer group support for disabled students, resulting in their inability to remain in mainstream institutions.
- *A Strict Curriculum:* Rigidity in the curriculum prevents exceptional students from learning on par with their peers. There is no unique curriculum available to meet the needs of exceptional students.

- *Pre-service education and professional development that is insufficient:* One of the major difficulties in inclusive education is a lack of training and professional development for mainstream teachers at all levels.
- *Lack of Infrastructure:* One of the major issues preventing us from realizing our dream of inclusive education is a lack of infrastructural amenities at our institution.
- *Negative Parental and Teacher Attitude:* One of the biggest issues in inclusive education is parents' and teachers' negative attitudes toward disabled, differently abled, and marginalized students.

Challenges in Inclusive Set-up

In India the number of the disabled people is so large, their problems so complex, available resources so scarce and social attitudes so damaging. The road to achieving inclusive education is a long and varied one, on which challenges and opportunities will arise. India is a multi-lingual, multi-cultural, multi-religious country, and its people are stratified along sharp socio-economic and caste lines. With an estimated 1,210 million people, India is the world's second most populated country after China. It has 17 per cent of the global population and 20 per cent of the world's out-of-school children. The aim of inclusion is to bring support to the students. The key purpose has become more challenging as schools accommodate students with increasingly diverse backgrounds and abilities.

The majority of schools in India are poorly designed and few are equipped to meet the unique needs of students with disabilities. It is also worth noting that there are challenges around procuring and resourcing for assistive devices. Despite various efforts for inclusive education in India, about 94 per cent of children with disabilities did not receive any educational services. Over and above some of these challenges that India shares with other developing countries are some distinctive features that will make the implementation of educational reform particularly difficult. The commitment of the Government of India to Universalization of Elementary Education (UEE) cannot be fully achieved without taking care of special educational needs of the physically and mentally challenged children. Inclusion is becoming a 'cannot' and doing the rounds in education circles but there are still a lot of cobwebs surrounding it.

The movement for inclusive education challenges the notion of business as usual for schools globally. Educational jurisdictions, whether situated in the so-called developing or developed worlds, are struggling with the complex relationships between schooling, exclusion and inclusion. A stubborn foe, exclusion is a seasoned traveler. Exclusion manifests in different forms according to geopolitical and cultural context. Accordingly, one would expect diverse interventions in order to dismantle its various formations.

- *Execution of Policy:* Concerned authorities must be serious and devoted enough to carry out policies addressing inclusive education, as well as to apply constitutional rights and provisions without regard to loopholes and technicalities.
- *Social Perception of Disability:* We must organize programmes to raise disability awareness and foster a positive social attitude toward differently abled and disenfranchised youngsters.
- *Increased parental awareness* : Such provisions and rights should be made known to the parents and families of such children through awareness programmes and advertisements in print and electronic media.
- *Skill-based instruction:* Trainees in mainstream teacher education centers should be taught how to deal with children like these.
- *Connecting together research and practise:* Universities and colleges are conducting disability-focused research and initiatives.
- *Peer mentoring:* Peer coaching is essential for improving teaching and learning in inclusive environments set up for education.

Prospects of Inclusive Education

A strategy for ensuring societal equality and making education universal, regardless of the learner's handicap, is inclusive education. It demonstrates how pupils with special needs can be included in regular classes without being segregated. With a focus on those who are disadvantaged and excluded, inclusive education is a developmental approach that attempts to address the educational needs of all kids, teens, and adults. The inclusion idea has received support from an increasing number of publications, policy papers, workshops, and other occasions. However, some groups and people are skeptical about whether a typical classroom can offer disabled children a decent education. Global disability organizations, international development organizations, intergovernmental organizations, and experts in the field of special and inclusive education have joined forces to form an alliance. All parties must fully involve individuals with disabilities and their families in the planning of all flagship activities in order to fulfill this goal. Encourage persons with disabilities and their families to participate fully in the development of local, national, regional, and international policies and guidelines governing the education of people with disabilities. Make sure that all governments, donors, and non-governmental organizations (NGOs) promote the fundamental right of all children, adolescents, and adults with disabilities to an education. Make regular classroom teachers' support for specialized teachers available, if at all possible. Because of this, we as educators — teachers, parents, and other stakeholders — must make it simpler to implement inclusive education as a philosophy grounded on human rights, rather than just as a curriculum.

Conclusion

It is challenging to promote inclusive education due to a variety of obstacles and problems in the educational system. With the right strategies and other methods, it is not difficult to succeed in inclusive education in the nation, but there are some concerns and challenges that we must carefully address. Regardless of educational level, all programmes must make it obligatory for teachers to receive the proper training, have a knowledge of and attitude toward impairments, and retain children who are different in order to make inclusion a reality (elementary, secondary, or higher). Each school needs more top-notch resources, teachers, and facilities if inclusive education programmes are to be successful.

References

Antil, N. (2014). Inclusive Education: Challenges and Prospects in India. *IOSR Journal of Humanities And Social Science*, *19*(9), 85-89.

Bhat, M.U.D., & Geelani, S.Z.A. (2007). Inclusive Education in India: Issues, Challenges, And Prospects. *Communications*.

Das, A.K., Kuyini, A.B., & Desai, I.P. (2013). Inclusive Education in India: Are the Teachers Prepared?. *International Journal of Special Education*, *28*(1), 27-36.

Essays, UK. (November 2013). The Importance and Definition of Inclusion Education Essay. Retrieved from https://www.ukessays.com/essays/education/the-importance-and-definition-ofinclusion-education-essay.php?cref=1

Hegarty, S., & Alur, M. (Eds.). (2002). *Education & Children with Special Needs: From Segregation to Inclusion*. Sage Publication.

Hudson, K. (2009), A qualitative investigation of white students' perceptions of diversity, *Journal of Diversity in Higher Education*, Vol. 2(3), Sep 149-155

Mary, M., & Thomas, S. (2013). Inclusive Education in Crossroads: Issues and Challenges. *Current Perspectives on Education*, 101.

Sanjeev, K., & Kumar, K. (2007). Inclusive education in India. *Electronic Journal for Inclusive Education*, *2*(2).

Sarao, T. (2016). Obstacles and challenges in inclusive education in India with special reference to teacher preparation. *Int. J. Educ. Appl. Res*, *6*, 6-35.

Shukla, Y. (2009). *Inclusive Growth in India: Challenges and Prospects*. Daly College, Indore.

Singh, J.D. (2016). Inclusive education in India — concept, need and challenges. *S. No. Paper Title Author Name Page No.*, 97.

Singh, Y.P., & Agarwal, A. (2015). Problems and prospects of inclusive education in India. *Global Summit on Education*, 181-191.

12

Overcoming Exclusion through Inclusive Approaches in Education

Anju Sharma*

Introduction

Inclusive education as an approach seeks to address the learning needs of all children, youth and adults with a specific focus on those who are vulnerable to marginalisation and exclusion. The principle of inclusive education was adopted at the Salamanca World Conference on Special Needs Education, UNESCO, 1994. Inclusive education means that "Schools should accommodate all children regardless of their physical, intellectual, social, emotional, linguistic or other conditions. This should include disabled and gifted children, street and working children, children from remote or nomadic populations, children from linguistic, ethnic or cultural minorities and children from other disadvantaged or marginalised areas or groups". Inclusion is seen as a process of addressing and responding to the diversity of needs of all learners through increasing participation in learning, cultures and communities, and reducing exclusion within and from education. It involves changes and modifications in content, approaches, structures and strategies, with a common vision which covers all children of the appropriate age range and a conviction that it is the responsibility of the regular system to educate all children.

Inclusive education is concerned with providing appropriate responses to the broad spectrum of learning needs in formal and non-formal educational settings. Rather than being a marginal theme on how some learners can be integrated in the mainstream education, inclusive education is an approach that looks into how to transform education systems in order to respond to the diversity of learners. It aims to enable both teachers and learners to feel comfortable with diversity and to see it as a challenge and enrichment in the learning environment, rather than a problem.

Need and Significance of the Implementation of Inclusion Policy

A policy of inclusion needs to be implemented in all schools and throughout Indian education system. The participation of all children needs to be ensured

*Assistant Professor, Khalsa College of Education, Amritsar

in all spheres of their life in and outside the school. Schools need to become centres that prepare children for life and ensure that all children, especially the differently abled children from marginalised sections, and children in difficult circumstances get the utmost benefit of this critical area of education. Opportunities to exhibit talents and share these with peers are powerful tools in fostering motivation and involvement among children.

It is a universal truth that all individuals are different basically from each other physically, mentally, educationally and socially up to a limit. All teachers, regardless of their experience and expertise face daily challenges from pupils who appear not to respond to their usual teaching approaches. One of the most interesting aspects of being a teacher is that new challenges appear all the time, and that this requires tenacity and professionalism in order to be successful. Teachers are needed to review continually their own work, and that the benefits of gaining new understanding and knowledge are a critical aspect of professionalism. Many children experience repeated disappointment and progress through school with a constant longing for recognition and peer approval. Excellence and ability may be singled out for appreciation, but at the same time opportunities need to be given to all children and their specific abilities need to be recognised and appreciated. This includes children with disabilities, who may need assistance or more time to complete their assigned tasks. It would be even better if, while planning for such activities, the teacher discusses them with all the children in the class, and ensures that each child is given an opportunity to contribute. When planning, therefore, teachers must pay special attention to ensuring the participation of all. This would become a marker of their effectiveness as teachers.

Policy Guidelines on Inclusion in Education

Children with disabilities are still combating obvious educational exclusion. Working children, those belonging to indigenous groups, rural populations and linguistic minorities, nomadic children and those affected by HIV and AIDS are other venerable groups. It is of crucial importance that all children and young people have access to education, it is equally important that they are able to take full part in school life and achieve desired outcome from their education experience. While subject-based academic performance is often used as an indicator of learning outcomes, "learning achievement" needs to be conceived as the acquisition of values, attitudes, knowledge and skills required to meet the challenges of contemporary societies. Promoting inclusion means encouraging positive attitudes and improving educational and social frameworks to cope with the new demands in educational structures and governance. It also involves improving inputs, processes and environment to foster learning, both at the level of the learner in his/her learning environment and at the system level to support the entire learning experience (UNESCO, 2007).

Some important steps in policy promotion of inclusive education should include:

a) Conducting a local situation analysis on the scope of the issue, available resources and their utilisation to support inclusion and inclusive education.
b) Mobilisation of opinion on the right of education for everybody.
c) Building of consensus around the concepts of inclusive and quality education.
d) Making legislation reforms to support inclusive education in line with international conventions, declarations and recommendations.
e) Supporting local capacity building to promote development towards inclusive education.
f) Developing ways of assessing the impact of inclusive and quality education.
g) Developing school and community based mechanisms to identify children not in school and find ways to help them enter school and remain there.
h) Helping teachers to understand their role in inclusive education and that inclusion of diversity in education is an opportunity and not a problem.
i) Eliminating legislative or constitutional barriers to disabled people being included in the mainstream education system.
j) Ensuring that education policies and strategies promote inclusive learning environments.
k) Initiating and facilitating national consultative processes, informed by international research, experience and standards, to develop national standards for inclusive education and for enhancing the quality of learning outcomes.

Approaches to Inclusive Education

It means challenging the status quo, removing curriculum barriers and presenting educational goals in interesting ways to engage all learners and serve all students equitably. In an inclusive education environment, all children, regardless of ability or disability, learn together in the same age-appropriate classroom. It is based on the understanding that all children and families are valued equally and deserve access to the same opportunities.

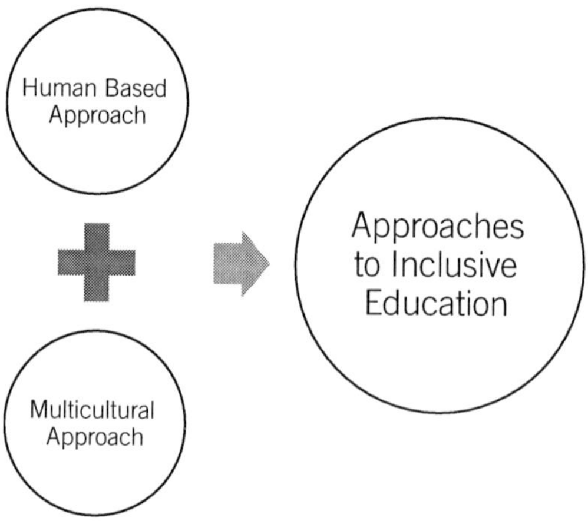

This section focuses on two approaches to Inclusive Education: the Human Right Based approach to inclusive education and the Multicultural Approach.

1) Human Right Based Approach

Many world governments have ratified the Convention on the Rights of the Child (CRC) a holistic human rights treaty addressing the social, economic, cultural, civic, and political and protection rights of children. It emphasises both the right to education on basis of equality of opportunity and the broad aims of education in terms of promoting the fullest possible development of the child. Article 2 of CRC gives governments an obligation to assure the realisation of all rights to every child without discrimination, including on the grounds of disability. Additionally, Article 23 of CRC specially addresses the right of children with disabilities to assistance to ensure that they are able to access education in a manner that promotes their social inclusion. The committee on child's rights identified four rights which must be understood as general principles to be applied in the realisation of all other rights:

a) Non-discrimination.
b) Best interest of the child.
c) Optimum development of the child.
d) The right of the child to be heard and taken seriously in accordance with age and maturity.

Article 24 of the 2006 Convention on the Rights of Persons with Disabilities (CRPD), which reaffirms the right of disabled children to quality education and committed governments to ensure that persons with disabilities can access an inclusive, quality and free primary education and secondary education on an equal basis with others in the communities in which they live. Article 32 places an obligation on donor governments to make their support inclusive of and accessible to persons with disabilities.

2) Multicultural Approach

Multicultural education describes a system of instruction that attempts to foster cultural pluralism and acknowledges the differences between races and cultures. It addresses the educational needs of a society that contains more than one set of traditions that is a mixture of many cultures. The goal of multicultural education is to help students understand and appreciate cultural differences and similarities and to recognise the accomplishments of diverse ethnic, racial, and socio-economic groups. It is a practice that hopes to transform the ways in which students are instructed by giving equal attention to the contributions of all the groups in a society. Multicultural education aims to eliminate prejudice, racism and all forms of oppression. To do this, "it is imperative that multicultural educators give voice and substance to struggles against oppression and develop the vision and the power of our future citizens to forge a more just society".

Goals of Multicultural Education

According to Hanley (2005), the goals are as follows:

a. To have every student achieve to his or her potential.
b. To learn how to learn and to think critically.
c. To encourage students to take an active role in their own education by bringing their stories and experiences into the learning scope.
d. To address diverse learning styles.
e. To appreciate the contributions of different groups who have contributed to our knowledge base.
f. To develop positive attitudes about groups of people who are different from ourselves.
g. To become good citizens of the school, the community, the country and the world community.
h. To learn how to evaluate knowledge from different perspectives.
i. To develop an ethnic, national and global identity.
j. To provide decision-making skills and critical analysis skills so the students can make better choices in their everyday lives.

Conclusion

Worldwide in education practice, there is a move to inclusive education policies emanating from the 1948 Universal Declaration of Human Rights. Many treaties, declarations and international conventions commit governments of countries to this. To realise this, a number of approaches have been adopted to promote inclusive education systems. Among them are the Human Rights Based approach and the Multicultural approach which have major implications to curriculum theory and practice in relation to curriculum design, content of curriculum, strategies of instruction, choice of resources, grouping of learners among others. To effectively implement inclusive education, the teacher factor should be taken into consideration as part of teacher development to instill necessary competencies that will support the teaching-learning process and promote development of all learners. At the highest level, inclusive education should be seen as a systematic change at all levels; principals, teachers, learners, school communities, policy makers, decision-makers, families, and society at large.

References

Bank, J.A. (1998). The lives and values of researchers. Implications for educating citizens in multicultural society. *Educational Researcher*, 4-17. (9)

Booth, M.T., & Unesco. (2003). *Overcoming exclusion through inclusive approaches in education: a challenge & a vision; conceptual paper*. Unesco.

Hanley, M.S. (2005). "The Scope of Multicultural Education". New Horizons for Learning. http://www.newhorizons.org/strategies/multicultural/hanley.htm

Hodge, S.R., Ammah, J.O.A., Casebolt, K., LaMaster, K., O'Sullivan, M. High school general physical education teachers' behaviors and beliefs associated with inclusion. *Sport, Education and Society*, 9 (3) 2004, 395-419.

Loreman, T. & Deppeler, J.M. (2001). Working towards full inclusion in education in Access. *The National Issues Journal for People with Disability*, 3(6), 5-8.

Sleeter, C. & Grant, C. (2008). *Making choices for multicultural education: five approaches to race, class, and gender*, New York: John Wiley, 2008.

UNESCO, The UNESCO Salamanca Statement and Framework for Action on Special Needs Education. (Paris: UNESCO, 1994) (1).

Wambugu, L. (2011). Overcoming Exclusion through Inclusive Education.

13

Challenges and Prospects in Inclusive Education

Baljit Kaur (Dr.)*

Introduction

Inclusive education stands for improvement of schools in all dimensions to address the educational needs of all children. Inclusive education has taken centre stage all over the world in recent decades, particularly in introducing educational reforms to prevent exclusionary practices. Inclusion has evolved over the past few decades as both a pedagogical strategy as well as political means to challenge exclusionary polices, laws and practices in the educational systems of countries. Inclusive education has students with disabilities having full membership in the age appropriate classes in their neighbourhood schools, with appropriate supplementary aids and support services (Lipsky & Gartner, 1999). Inclusive education is a highly contentious issue fraught with debates and conflict; however, focus on it has produced a vast body of knowledge through research and teaching. More generally, social, economic and political inclusion of persons with disabilities is now a part of the international human rights movement, which has been emerging and developing throughout the 20th century (Rioux, 2001). Education for the disabled has become a matter of entitlement — a fundamental human right — rather than a privilege or charity. Around the globe, governments are increasingly viewing the rights of their citizens in a manner consistent thinking about disability linked to this trend. The older way of viewing disability as a matter of deviance, deficiency or disease — the pathology of an individual or family failing to attain standard of normalcy — persist in some spheres, but these views are being replaced by social construct in many regions. It is increasingly common today for disability to be viewed as pathology of society, as a matter of environment and social failure rather than through the previous lens of an individual's limitations. This new framework of human rights sets the stage for countries to support social well-being for their citizens (Alur et al. 2000; Rioux, 2001). With the release of the Salamanca Statement in 1994 (UNESCO), a large number of developing countries started

*Assisstant Professor, Khalsa College of Education, G.T. Road, Amritsar

reformulating their policies to promote the inclusion of students with disabilities into mainstream schools. While a large number of developed countries now have policies or laws promoting "inclusive education", a number of developing countries continue to provide educational services to students with disabilities in "segregated" schools. Typically, inclusive education means "that students with disabilities are served primarily in the general education settings, under the responsibility of regular classroom teacher. When necessary and justifiable, students with disabilities may also receive some of their instruction in another setting, such as resource room" (Mastropieri & Scruggs, 2004). The main focus of New Education Policy 2020 is equity and inclusion in education. Inclusion involves rearrangement of the whole system with the aim of ensuring the wide range of educational opportunities in the fields of higher or school education. This includes curriculum, pedagogy of school subjects and recreational opportunities, etc. The policy is framed to avoid segregation and isolation of ethnic and linguistic minorities, those with disabilities and also those who face learning difficulties due to language barriers and are at the risk of educational exclusion. We make sense of the world through language and this creates and recreates power, authority and also legitimation. NEP 2020 has set the goal for inclusion to be authoritative with the different languages at different steps of education.

Problems of Inclusive Education in India

Inclusive education is a big priority for Government of India. However, a wide gap in the policies and practices exists in the country with respect to inclusive education. There are a number of problems that interfere in proper practice of inclusive education in our country. These barriers are explained as under.

a. Skilled teachers — Skills of teachers which are responsible for implementing inclusive education are also not up to as desired and necessary for inclusion. Researchers examined the current skill levels of regular primary and secondary school teachers in Delhi, India in order to teach students with disabilities in inclusive education settings. They reported that nearly 70% of the regular school teachers had neither received training in special education nor had any experience teaching students with disabilities. The majority of school personnel in India are not trained to design and implement educational programmes for students with disabilities in regular schools. Most teacher training programmes in India do not have a unit on Disability Studies (Myreddi & Narayan, 2000). Finally, although both primary and secondary school teachers rated themselves as having limited or low competence for working with students with disabilities, there was no statistically significant difference between their perceived skill levels.

b. Attitudes towards inclusion —Attitudes towards inclusion and disability among teachers, administrators, parents, peers and policy planners. In addition to many other requirements towards inclusion and disability among teachers, parents, peers, administrators and policy planners for implementation of inclusive education need positive attitudes towards inclusion. However, negative attitudes are still persisting among these in many cases. There is evidence that when parents are knowledgeable and supportive of integrated education, they tend to have a positive effect on school personnel (U. Sharma, 2001). Teachers and parents attitudes may contribute to remove barrier to successful inclusive practices.

c. Lack of awareness — At all levels, lack of basic awareness about children with disabilities hinder the practices. They have their own notions i.e. socially and culturally constructed notions about certain obvious disabilities but lack scientific and educational knowledge about the disabilities such as classification, labelling, special needs and adaptations etc.

d. Improper curriculum adaptation — For practising inclusive education, curricular adaptations suited to special and unique needs of every learner, including children with disabilities, are necessary. Concepts like 'Universal Instructional Design' are to be properly developed and incorporated into the curriculum. However, needed curricular adaptations are either missing altogether or are improper.

e. School environment including difficulties in physical access — School environment needs accommodations for truly practising inclusive education. However, such accommodations are not there in majority of the schools. Facilities like ramps, lifts, and directional cues etc. are mostly absent in schools.

f. Insufficient and improper pre-service teacher education — The pre-service teacher education programmes being run in the country are failing to sensitise and equip prospective teachers in inclusive education practices. Changes are needed to make these teacher education programmes more effective. Currently, teacher education programmes producing special teachers are controlled by Rehabilitation Council of India whereas these producing general teachers are controlled by National Council for Teacher Education. These two apex bodies need to collaborate and devise measures for producing skilled teachers capable of implementing inclusive education.

g. Negative self-perceptions of children with disabilities — For practising inclusive education, negative self-perceptions of children with disabilities pose a great challenge. These negative perceptions are often strengthened by neighbours, peers, and teachers. Without wiping out these negative self-perceptions, true inclusion of such children is not possible. Many religious institutions and temple trusts have misconception about disabilities, because they consider the disability to be the result of a person's misdeeds in his previous life.

h. ICT availability and related competencies — Present age is the age of information and communication technology (ICT). ICT is providing great help in almost all endeavours of human life including education and training.

There are a number of ICT-enabled pedagogical and assistive devices available particularly useful for children with disabilities. Their use can ease and expedite inclusive education. These should be made available and competencies for their use should be developed among all stakeholders.

i. Improper policy planning and lack-luster implementation—Government of India claims that it has implemented inclusive education everywhere and at all levels. However, the policy planning is improper and measures to assess the degree of implementation have not been developed. Furthermore, implementation of inclusive education in private sector has not been enforced and ensured. A large number of school personnel are also not aware of funding available to include students with disabilities in regular schools. There is some evidence that those educators who are knowledgeable about government policies and laws concerning integrated education tend to have positive attitudes toward implementing such programmes (U. Sharma, 2001).

j. Funding—Adequate funding is a necessity for inclusion and yet it is rare. Schools often lack adequate facilities, qualified and properly-trained teachers and other staff members, educational materials and general support. Sadly, lack of resources is pervasive throughout many educational systems.

To promote inclusive values, acceptance of individual and cultural differences must be included in all curricula, not solely within special education. The future of a truly inclusive education relies on a cultural shift that supports and nurtures differences, and views success through a lens not focused on standardisation but on diversity. The Index for Inclusion has been utilised worldwide to support schools, to remove perceived barriers and to establish increasingly inclusive school cultures and practices. The Index aids in the creation of a culture that is dedicated to identifying and reducing barriers to inclusion and increases the learning and participation for all students. In order to overcome the deficit view upon which the current understanding of inclusion is based, we must avoid segregation and discrimination as we meet specialised educational needs. A start in this direction is to change the language and the lens through which we view inclusion. We need to seize all opportunities to work against this development. Global efforts to face future needs in teacher and school building leadership education include fostering dispositions that view diversity as an enriching aspect of classrooms. The challenge is to train professionals who are proficient in educating a diverse group of students while creating a classroom culture of acceptance and respect for all. To do this, we must begin with teacher and school building leadership training programmes.

School Leadership Training Programme

Training of Teachers: If integrated education is to become a reality in India, then the training of teachers has to become a top priority. The educational authorities in India may adopt a policy of training one teacher from each school or a cluster of schools. The teacher would need to be provided with intensive training to work with various disabilities and could then act as an integration specialist or an inclusion facilitator for one or a number of schools located in close proximity. Also in-service teachers would need continued training to update their skills and knowledge of integrated education strategies. Jangira and Ahuja (1993) reported that as a result of improved programme planning and better management skills now made available to the teachers, the capacity of various states to implement integration programmes was enhanced. Both regular school teachers and students became more receptive toward students with disabilities (Azad, 1996). About 13,000 children with disabilities received educational services in regular schools (Azad, 1996). More than 9,000 teachers received training to work with disabled students in integrated settings (Azad, 1996). It is clear that regular school educators need training in issues related to the implementation of integrated education.

Need to design innovative system of training — Several authors have cautioned that India will not be able to successfully implement integrated educational services unless regular school educators are trained at mass scale. Comments on this situation as follows: "the number of persons who need training is very large and the conventional training methods cannot simply meet the requirements." Therefore, there is a need to design some innovative models to train educators at mass level. One possibility to educate such a large number of teachers is by using Distance Open Learning or DOL. Indira Gandhi National Open University (IGNOU) has a history of successfully running courses for a larger number of students using DOL mode. IGNOU, in association with Rehabilitation Council of India, is considering offering various courses to the trainers of children with disabilities, including teachers. It is expected that such training, accompanied with ongoing in-service training, would prove very useful for school educators.

Need for collaboration between different ministries — Different ministries in India administer various services for persons with disabilities (Alur, 2001). For example, while "integrated education" is the responsibility of Ministry of Human Resource Development (Ministry of Education), education in special schools is the responsibility of Ministry of Social Justice and Empowerment. This is just one example of the waste of already limited resources. India cannot afford to have such administrative arrangements. There is a need for streamlining administrative arrangements so that funds provided to different ministries for persons with disabilities can be used effectively.

Involve NGO's in implementing integrated education programmes — There are more than one million NGO's working in India (Canadian International Development Agency, 2003). Although not all of them are working in the education sector, a large number still provide educational services to children with disabilities. These organisations can play a significant role in implementing integrated education because they are widely located in India and can serve both urban and rural school communities. Unfortunately, a large majority of NGOs still believe that segregated education is the best way to educate students with disabilities (Alur, 2001). It would, therefore, be necessary to train the key stakeholders in these NGO's about the benefits of integrated education as well as practical aspects of implementing integrated education in regular schools.

Establish an alternate system of examination — Most school educators in India are concerned that integration of students with disabilities would result in lowering school standards because these students would not be able to pass exams (U. Sharma & Desai, 2002). This seems to be a genuine concern of teachers because it can influence their promotion. Thus, it is necessary to establish an alternative system of examination for students with disabilities. Such an examination system is already in practice in the USA. Students in this system are asked to do activities that demonstrate their abilities rather than disabilities. It is expected that teachers in India would feel more comfortable including students with disabilities in their classrooms if such a system existed.

Conclusion

Inclusive education will require additional funding, but even more importantly, it requires the change of old and outdated attitudes. Over and above some of these challenges that India shares with other developing countries are some distinctive features that will make the implementation of educational reform particularly difficult. India is a multilingual, multicultural, multireligious country, and its people are stratified along sharp socio-economic and caste lines. Therefore, unless the challenges are not carefully identified and systematically addressed by the society, inclusion will remain a policy on paper. So, there is a need to design some innovative models to implement inclusive education at mass level.

References

Alur, M. (2001). Inclusion in the Indian Context. *Humanscape, 8*(6), 1-8.

Alur, M. & Rioux, M. (2001). Disability and social justice. In Alur, M. & Timmons, V. *Inclusive Education Across Cultures*: New Delhi, Sage Publications.

Azad, Y.A. (1996). *Integration of disabled in common schools: A survey-study of IEDC in the country.* New Delhi: National Council of Educational Research and Training.

Jangira, N.K., & Ahuja, A. (1993). Special education in India. *Asia Appraiser* (October-December), 6-11.

Lipsky & Gartner, 1999). Inclusive Education. In Alur, M. & Timmons, V. *Inclusive Education Across Cultures*: New Delhi, Sage Publications.

Mastropieri, M.A., & Scruggs, T.E. (2004). *The inclusive classroom: Strategies for effective instruction.* NY: Pearson.

Myreddi, V., & Narayan, J. (2000). Preparation of special education teachers: Present status and future trends. *Asia Pacific Disability Rehabilitation Journal, 10* (1), 1-8.

Rioux, M. (2001). Socio Political aspects of disability in Canada. *Human Rights And Inclusive Education in India.* Unpublished paper presented at north south dialogue on inclusive education conference held at national resource centre for inclusion, Mumbai

Sharma, U (2005). Integrated Education in India: Challenges and Prospects. *Disability Studies Quarterly, 25 (1) retrieved on 25 Feb. 2016 from http://dsq-sds.org/article/view/524/701*

Sharma, U., & Desai, I. (2002). Measuring concerns about integrated education in India. *Asia and Pacific Journal on Disability,* 5(1), 2-14.

Sharma, U. (2001). *The attitudes and concerns of school principals and teachers regarding the integration of students with disabilities into regular schools in India.* Unpublished Ph.D. Thesis, University of Melbourne, Melbourne.

14

Inclusive Education
Various Classroom Strategies

Triptjit Kaur Arora*

Introduction

Inclusive education is a recent concept which means schools for creating effective classroom functioning where the educational needs of all children including those with disabilities are addressed. Inclusive education is not only concerned with differently abled children or finding an alternative to segregated special schools. This education signifies the dictum "children who learn together, learn to live together". It indicates the education of all children with all others regardless of their strengths and weaknesses. Different important classroom strategies are an inherent quality of inclusive education. These strategies can be used in the schools for the students with mild to severe special needs. In inclusive classroom, it is important that the teacher should understand the learning needs, social and physical needs of the students. So there is proper need of effective classroom management and strategies.

Good classroom strategies are part of inclusive education. Different important classroom strategies such as Collaborative Teaching, Cooperative Learning and Peer Tutoring etc. can be used to make inclusive education effective.

Teaching Strategies

Collaborative Teaching — Collaborative teaching is an innovative pedagogical approach. It helps to achieve a common goal of teaching while working together. Special teachers come to common classroom as co-teacher with general teachers and contribute their knowledge to make learning easy and effective. Inclusive classroom requires the collaboration of a wide range of professionals, regular teachers, special teachers, counselor and therapists etc.

The most important benefit of this approach is that it provides chance to every student to work with different students and establish a significant working

*Assistant Professor, PCM SD College for Women, Jalandhar

relationship with each other. Thus, collaborative teaching approach is an effective approach to provide good environment to the learners to learn together in a common classroom. It also provides an expanded number of teaching styles that may connect with more students and faculty to benefit from the healthy exchange of ideas. But for successful collaboration, teachers must learn how to communicate clearly and how to resolve conflicts in teaching.

Cooperative Learning — Where the normal students are studying with the exceptional children then cooperative learning is successful for all the children. Cooperative learning is an important educational approach which aims to arrange the classroom activities into academic and social learning experiences. Cooperative learning is a teaching method where students of mixed level of ability are arranged into the groups and proceed towards common educational objectives. Thus, students learn to work with all types of children. They learn to relate to their peers and other learners as they work together in a group. Thus, each student can gain the opportunity to contribute in small groups. Various important skills e.g. interpersonal and collaborative skills can be learned.

Peer Tutoring — Peer tutoring was coined by Kenneth Bruffee. It is not a new idea. It is an instructional method in which one child tutor teaches another child. It is a method in which same age or older children help to support each other in learning. Peer tutoring is often used in classroom as recommended inclusion strategy for students with disabilities. Students with disabilities need special efforts and peer tutoring helps the learner and encourage them towards learning. It also develops more positive self-esteem among all the students with disability if they are assigned as tutor. This strategy also contributes towards gaining a deeper understanding of subjects. Peer tutoring is important to make learning more effective and interesting. It can develop many essential skills and helps to socialise the child. Miller and Miller also said that "Peer tutoring is an economically and educationally effective intervention of person with disabilities that can benefit both the tutor and tutee, socially and educationally by motivating them to learn." There are various types of peer tutoring such as unidirectional, bi-directional, cross-age peer tutoring, peer assisted learning strategies, reciprocal peer tutoring and same-age peer tutoring. Any type of peer tutoring can be used according to the students and all students are involved. Thus, it helps to identify the students with disabilities and who have the problem of paying attention and have emotional imbalance.

Apart from this, many other new technologies have been developed, in which one is ICT. This form of technology has come as a boon in the field of education. By using this in the field of inclusive education, education can be made easy, interesting and all type of children can be educated together without any discrimination.

Conclusion

The use of ICT is well recognised in the educational stream. ICT provides support in education and removes barriers for the children to participate in learning. It helps the students with special educational needs to keep contact with their classroom. ICT helps learner to learn at their pace. In current education system, education fulfills the needs of students with disability as well as socially disadvantaged group. It can be integral in supporting learner in a variety of ways within inclusive setting. Technology can help disabled children to overcome many of their communication difficulties. These technologies contribute to effectiveness of educational process by enabling students with disabilities to actively participate in learning.

In this way, inclusive education can be made effective with different classroom strategies and new techniques. There need is to put them to good use. For this, along with general teacher, a special teacher also should be appointed.

References

Dash. N., (2006), *Inclusive Education*, Atlantic Publisher.

Kaur, R. & Singh, A., (2020), *Inclusive Education*, S.G. Publisher, Jalandhar.

Mangal, S.K. & Mangal, S., (2019), *Creating an Inclusive School*, PHI Learning.

Singh, A. & Virk, K.J. (2016), *Inclusive Education*, Twenty First Century Publication.

Sahu, B.K. (2002), *Education of the Exceptional Children*, New Delhi.

15

Inclusive Education
A Journey to Equitable Education

Amandeep Kaur*

Introduction

The term 'Inclusive education' has become a buzz phrase in the field of education of children with special needs. Inclusive education has its roots in education of differently abled children. Inclusive Education is based on the principle of Inclusion of all children under one roof irrespective of their disabilities. It focuses on the idea of 'togetherness' means that all children should learn together in a classroom. Inclusive Schools must recognise the individuality of the child and respond according to the needs of the child. Inclusive schools must provide appropriate educational set up and accommodate both learning styles and speed of learning. The first World Conference on Education for All was held in Thailand in 1990. In this Conference, the focus was on acknowledging that a large number of marginalised groups and children with disability were excluded from educational system worldwide. So a number of movements and actions have been adopted by different commissions and committees at local and world level for providing quality and equitable education to all on the ground of human rights. It is quite important that meaning of Inclusive education is not to be conceived in terms of add-on in mainstreaming education. Inclusive education should be implemented in whole school approach. It aims at increasing participation of learners in schools and minimising the effect of barriers and restructuring of educational system from normalisation to full inclusion. Full inclusion refers to the situation where all individuals regardless of any kind of handicap and severity of handicap are included in full classroom (Mastropieri & Scruggs, 2000). Inclusive education is about bringing and implementing changes for education of all. Basically, inclusive education is related to transformation of educational system as a whole.

---

*Assistant Professor, Khalsa College of Education, Amritsar

What does Inclusion include?

- Inclusion is a process by which a state or school attempts to include and respond all children irrespective of their disability as individuals.
- Emphasises the effectiveness of school activities.
- Emphasises on reconstruction of curriculum and restructuring of educational system.

Barriers in Inclusive Education

Barriers in inclusive education are not only at organisational setup and academic level. There are two types: intrinsic and extrinsic barriers that create hindrance in the way of education for all. These barriers are:

Intrinsic Barriers	*Extrinsic Barriers*
• Hesitation	• Attitude of society and teachers
• Fear and awkwardness	• Unorganised educational setup
• Low self-concept	• Unhealthy attitude of peer group
• Low self-efficacy	• Lack of medical facilities
• Attitude to disability	• Non availability of equipment
• Lack of confidence	• Expectation of society
• Dependency on parents	• Curricular barriers

A Journey to Equitable Education

Inclusive education gives a message

Every child belongs to school.
Every child is welcomed in the school.

Inclusive education provides such a type of classroom environment where students with special needs spend most of their time with non-disabled students. Differently abled students are educated in inclusive settings without any discrimination. In India, education for children with special needs is still provided in segregated settings. Inclusive education can become a journey to equitable education only when society will develop a positive attitude towards children with special needs. Society must accept the child having any kind of disability. An individual must be considered as human being. He must not be categorised or labeled as able or disabled child. Every individual has some kind of latent talent in him. Inclusive education provides an educational setting in which abilities of the child are utilised properly and positive attitude is developed among the students. Inclusive education facilitates retention of students in the school and it focuses on placement of children from special and segregated schools into regular schools. The optimistic picture of inclusive education indicates that policies and practices in the field of special education have improved overtime. It shows that the attitude of society towards less fortunate children has changed with the passage of time. A number of problems are in the way of journey of inclusive education. These problems are:

- *Receptive attitude of society:* A long time ago and in early societies, disabled children were killed by their parents because these were considered as unfortunate and not perfect according to social norms. It was also assumed that a disabled child is the result of anger of god or the parents of disabled child have done some kind of sin that is why they got such a child. Parents usually felt guilty and they took the blame for differences and impairment on themselves.
- *Segregation of students from regular classrooms:* Segregated institutions and mainstreamed schools for children with special needs continued to grow in numbers and size during the late 19th century. Setting of special rooms in regular schools has changed the mindset of society. At the end of 19th century, public attitude about the place of individuals with disabilities in schools began to change. Segregation of disabled children from the regular classrooms creates feeling of inferiority among the students. They assume themselves as a burden on the parents and society. Sometimes such a feeling may lead to development of severe psychological problems and suicidal tendencies among differently abled children.
- *Dumping of children in regular classroom:* Inclusion does not mean dumping of children in regular classrooms. A number of Acts have been implemented by Government of India for persons with disability. But the major concern of most of schools is only to adopt the law and not to adapt the school settings for the children with special needs. Only posters and flexes are hanged on the walls of schools and no congenial and healthy environment is provided by schools.

The United Nations Charter on Rights of Child stated that every child has a right to education and right to make progress and denial to give education means denial the rights of child.

Path of Inclusion: From Segregation to Empowerment

Julka (2001) has traced the path of inclusion in the following way:

Segregation ▼ Integration ▼ Inclusion ▼ Empowerment

The path of inclusion of differently abled children has progressed from segregation in special schools to inclusion in regular schools. Inclusive education aims at empowerment of all children having disabilities so that they can perform academic tasks properly and it also aims at developing functional and academic skills among students. Development of skills will make them independent and they will not be dependent on others for their daily activities.

All the countries in the world have done tremendous efforts for proper organisation and implementation of support services in schools. Earlier efforts were being made to provide support to children with special needs and it was considered only cognitive and physical impairment. However, current trends in the field of inclusive education point towards the inclusion of marginalised groups in terms of socio-economic status and cultural differences. The drive towards inclusion of children with special needs in regular classroom is fuelled by a number of initiatives and policies and treaties as:

Movements towards Inclusive Education in World

Conference / Movement	*Main Theme*
UNESCO Convention Against Discrimination in Education, 1960	Prohibit any exclusion from educational opportunities on the basis of any type of differences. UNESCO aims at promoting inclusive education system and removes those barriers that hinder the participation of students in daily life activities.
Integrated Education for Disabled Children, UNICEF, 1986.	To strengthen the integration of differently abled children in regular classrooms.
UN Convention on Rights of the Child	Equal rights to all children
First World Conference, Thailand, 1995	Education for all
South African Movement, 1996	Social restructuring and democratisation educational transformation in South Africa
National Commission on Special Needs in Education and Training, 1996	Research was conducted on services that was provided to differently abled children
National Committee on Educational Support Services, 1996	To research ways to address the diverse needs of children in educational setup
White paper on Education and Training, 1995	It was based on theme of transformation of education system into single system and non-discriminatory practices in education.
Integrated National Disability Strategy	Provide employment and training opportunities and educational support services for learners with disabilities.
The Salamanca Statement, 1994.	To provide unique opportunity to place Special Education in wider framework of school and Education system.
World Conference on Special Needs Education, 1994.	Inclusive education emerged as a reform and gained momentum due to this conference.
Dakar Framework for Action, 2000	Education system should respond flexibly for retaining children from marginalised groups in schools.
New Policy on Inclusive Education, Namibia, 2014	To provide access, equity and quality education to all children. It also supports rights-based approach to inclusive education. Right to Education is right of every child.

Movements towards Inclusive Education in India

Conference / Movement	*Main Theme*
Article 45 of Indian Constitution, 1950	No individual of India shall be deprived of his life except according to laws established by Jurisdiction.
Kothari Education Commission, 1964	According to this commission, experimentation in integrated programmes is urgently required and every attempt should be made to bring as many children into the integrated educational system.
National Policy on Education, 1986	This policy stresses upon the idea that once the children with disabilities acquire basic skills, which would be learned in resource room, then these students should be mainstreamed.
86th amendment of Indian Constitution, 2002	Free and compulsory Education to all children between ages 6-14 years.
National Policy for People with Disabilities, 2006.	Main concern of this policy was to bridge the gap between rural and urban areas by creating more District Disability and Rehabilitation centres.
Persons with Disability Act, 1995	Equal opportunities for people with disabilities
Right to Education Act, 2009	Right to free and compulsory education to all including those with disabilities, at a neighbourhood school.
The Rights of Persons with Disabilities Act, 2016	This act focuses on non-discrimination, equality of opportunity and full participation of persons with disability in society.

A new concept has been introduced in the area of inclusive education, i.e. Universal design for learning. This design aims at maximising access for all learners in schools. Universal design for learning is based on the principles of flexibility and tolerance for error.

Inclusive education progressively became a national and global movement. Although we have crossed a number of milestones in the way of inclusive education but journey to this destination is never ending. However, equity in Inclusive setting is big question as number of notions and social dilemmas are there in the society. We cannot implement inclusive education in vacuum. Socio-economic factors and historical perspective have an effect on the policies and acts. A lot of efforts are still required on the part of governments, NGO's and general public.

References

Alkahtani, M.A. (2016). Review of literature on children with special needs. *Journal of Education and Practice*, 7 (35).

Balikci, S. & Rapap, S. (2017). Embedded instruction to teach functional skills to a preschool child with autism. *International Journal of Developmental Disabilities,* 63(I), 17-26.

Bishnu, S. (2017). Policies for developing inclusive education: A review. *International Journal of Advanced Research and Innovative Ideas in Education,* 3*(*3), 3312-3319.

Collins, T. S. (2010). *Functional communication training to increase communication skills for young children with autism spectrum order*. A Dissertation presented to the graduate School of Clemson University.

Dash, N. (2012). *Inclusive Education for Children with Special needs*. New Delhi: Atlantic Publishers.

Singh, J.D. (2016). Inclusive education in India — concept, need and challenges. *Scholarly Research Journal for Humanity Science and English Languages,* 3(13), 322-329.

Singh, V. (2016). Ensuring social inclusion and quality in learning of children with special needs through inclusive teacher education. *Scholarly Research Journal for Interdisciplinary Studies,* 6(33), 260-266.

Websites

www.liste.org
www.ncert.in
www.specialneeds.com
www.staffs.org

16

Overcoming Exclusion through Inclusive Approaches in Education

Jyotpreet Kaur (Dr.)*

Introduction

Inclusive education is when all students, regardless of any challenges they may have, are placed in age-appropriate general education classes that are in their own neighbourhood to receive high-quality instruction, interventions, and supports that enable them to meet success in the core curriculum. Inclusive education is not only an implementation of a legalised programme of education, but inclusive education is primarily an attitude, a value and a belief system, not merely a set-up of actions. The word 'include' implies being a part of something, being embraced into whole. Inclusive education means different and diverse students learning side by side in the same classroom. They enjoy field trips and after-school activities together. They attend the same sports meets and plays.

The school and classroom operate on the premise that students with disabilities are as fundamentally competent as students without disabilities. Therefore, all students can be full participants in their classrooms and in the local education community. Much of the movement is related to legislation that students receive their education in the least restrictive environment. This means they are with their peers without disabilities to the maximum degree possible, with general education the placement of first choice for all students.

Successful inclusive education happens primarily through accepting, understanding, and attending to student differences and diversity, which can include physical, cognitive, academic, social and emotional. The driving principle is to make all students feel welcomed, appropriately challenged, and supported in their efforts.

Inclusive education ensures that all students attend and are welcomed by their neighbourhood schools in age-appropriate, regular classes and are supported to learn, contribute and participate in all aspects of the life of the school. Inclusive education is about how we develop and design our schools, classrooms, programmes and activities so that all students learn and participate

*Assistant Professor, Khalsa College of Education, G. T. Road, Amritsar

together. Neighbourhood schools are the heart of our communities, and Inclusion believes they are essential for a quality inclusive education system.

Around the world, children are excluded from schools where they belong because of disability, race, language, religion, gender, and poverty. But every child has the right to be supported by their parents and community to grow, learn, and develop in the early years, and upon reaching school age, to go to school and be welcomed and included by teachers and peers alike. When all children, regardless of their differences, are educated together, everyone benefits, this is the cornerstone of inclusive education.

According to UNICEF: To close the education gap for children with disabilities there should be work to promote inclusive education. UNICEF supports government efforts to foster and monitor inclusive education systems. It focuses on four key areas as Advocacy, Awareness-raising, Capacity-building, Implementation support. It promotes inclusive education in discussions, high-level events and other forms of outreach geared towards policymakers and the general public. It shines a spotlight on the needs of children with disabilities by conducting research and hosting roundtable talks, workshops and other events for government partners. It builds the capacity of education systems in partner countries by training teachers, administrators and communities, and providing technical assistance.

Inclusive education values diversity and the unique contribution each student brings to the classroom. In a truly inclusive setting, every child feels safe and has a sense of belonging. Students and their parents participate in setting learning goals and take part in decisions that affect them and school staff have the training, support, flexibility, and resources to nurture, encourage, and respond to the needs of all students. Inclusive education – also called inclusion – is education that includes everyone, with non-disabled and disabled people (including those with "special educational needs") learning together in mainstream schools, colleges and universitics.

According to the Principal Secretary to the Prime Minister, one of the important objective of the NEP 2020 is inclusive education. NEP 2020 is also focused on primary and pre-primary education and has the aim of inclusive education, learning and new knowledge, Inclusive and Equitable Education System by 2030.

According to NEP 2020 (6. 6.1); Equitable and Inclusive Education: Learning for All Education is the single greatest tool for achicving social justice and equality. Inclusive and equitable education — while indeed an essential goal in its own right — is also critical to achieving an inclusive and equitable society in which every citizen has the opportunity to dream, thrive and contribute to the nation. The education system must aim to benefit India's children so that no child loses any opportunity to learn and excel because of circumstances of birth or background. This policy reaffirms that bridging the social category gaps in access, participation and learning outcomes in school education will continue to be one of the major goals of all education sector development programmes. This means the system must adapt to include Disabled people. SEDGs should not have to adapt to the system. The education system must recognise that it creates barriers for Disabled learners, for instance if parts of the school are inaccessible. Disabled pupils and students may require adaptations and support to access the curriculum.

According to NEP 2020 (14.14.2); Equity and Inclusion in Higher Education: The dynamics and also many of the reasons for exclusion of SEDGs (Socio-economically disadvantaged groups) from the education system are common across school and higher education sectors. Therefore, the approach to equity and inclusion must be common across school and higher education. For Equity and higher education additional actions that are specific to higher education shall be adopted by all governments and HEIs. NEP (14.4)

Inclusive Education Approaches

There is a definite need for teachers to be supported in implementing an inclusive classroom.

Use a Variety of Instructional Formats

Start with whole-group instruction and transition to flexible groupings which could be small groups, and paired learning with peer group. With regard to the whole group, using technology such as interactive whiteboards is related to high student engagement. Regarding flexible groupings: for younger students, these are often teacher-led but for older students, they can be student-led with teacher monitoring. Peer-supported learning can be very effective and engaging and take the form of pair-work, cooperative grouping, peer tutoring, and student-led demonstrations.

Ensure Access to Academic Curricular Content

All students need the opportunity to have learning experiences in line with the same learning goals. This will necessitate thinking about what supports individual need, but overall strategies are making sure all students hear instructions, that they do indeed start activities, that all students participate in large group instruction, and that students' transition in and out of the classroom at the same time.

Apply Universal Design for Learning

These are methods that are varied and that support many learners' needs. They include multiple ways of representing content to students and for students to represent learning back, such as images, models, objects, graphic organisers, oral and written responses, and technology. These can also be adapted as modifications for inclusion where they have large print, use headphones, are allowed to have a peer write their dictated response, draw a picture instead, use calculators, or just have extra time for specially abled. The power of project-based and inquiry learning where students individually or collectively investigate an experience can be explored.

Use Supportive Media

Textbooks are often accompanied by workbook, CDs and cassettes, videos, CDROM and comprehending teaching guides, which provide a rich and varied resource for teachers and learners. Inclusive education can be enhanced by the use of supportive media for specially abled, physically handicapped or excluded groups.

Make curriculum more inclusive and develop Institutional Development Plan that contains specific plans for action on increasing participation from SEDGs, including but not limited to the mentioned terms in NEP 2020 (14.4.2e and m)

Case Study

Case study offers a means of investigation of complex social units consisting of multiple variables of potential importance in understanding the phenomenon (Merriam 1988). Case studies can be a step towards making curriculum more inclusive and can help in developing specific plans to enhance participation from SEDGs.

Steps of Case study

1. Determine and define research questions:
   Research question in the present case study was — Does inclusive education show any impact on the performance of handicapped child in reading and reflecting of text?
2. Select cases and determine data collection and analysis techniques.
3. In the present study a physically handicapped child was observed. Data was collected using in-class observation and performance analysis.
4. Preparation for data collection and collection of data in the field.
5. Data was collected during regular classroom teaching.
6. Evaluate and analyse data.
7. Data was analysed by calculating number of errors before and after classroom teaching. Errors reduced from 60% to 20%.
8. Prepare the report.
9. The case study was analysed and final report was prepared.

A case study was conducted on the subject named Arshdeep Singh, student of B.Ed Sem 1, Sec A (2022), K.C.E, G.T. Road, Amritsar. He is a

Evaluation of Case Study	*Teacher's Role*	*Participant Subject/Student's role*
Before Class	* Prepares for class- explanation of reading skills * Consults colleagues * Assigns topics for reading: The Summit Within Class VIII English	* Prepares individually * Discusses in small group * Provides case/subjects initial data and entry level information
During Class	* Deals with readings * Leads case discussion * Checks pronunciation, speed, vocabulary, summary of topic. * We can overcome any obstacle or situation in life if we have endurance, persistence and will power.	* Raises questions regarding readings * Participates in discussion
After Class	* Evaluates and records student participation-% age of errors was calculated. * Evaluates materials and updates students reading skills and reflection on topics read	* Compares personal performance with peer group * Reviews class discussion for reading and reflecting on texts

physically handicapped student. His performance in the subject of Reading and Reflecting on Texts showed improvement using inclusive education approaches. Chapter 5 of Class VIII English Main Course book – The Summit Within in which the narrator Major HPS Ahluwalia shares his experiences and describes his feelings of standing on top of the highest mountain in the world, Mighty Mount Everest was considered for case study reading skill analysis. Before Inclusive Education, the child had poor reading skills, poor decoding skills, poor reading fluency, poor pronunciation, slow reading rate, difficulty in grammar and vocabulary skills.

Case study showed that after Inclusive Education, the child showed improvement in reading skills. The student was able to read and reflect the textbook. The student was able to read to activate and reinforce reading skills. The student was able to do reading and can put into practice grammatical structure, new items and elements of pronunciation similar to oral dialogue, short competitions and listening activities.

Inclusive systems provide a better quality education for all children and is instrumental in changing discriminatory attitudes. Schools provide the context for a child's first relationship with the world outside their families, enabling the development of social relationships and interactions. Respect and understanding grow when students of diverse abilities and backgrounds play, socialise, and learn together. These communities start at school, where all students learn to live alongside peers. They learn together; they play together; they grow and are nurtured together. A subject teacher can address the challenges and succeed in using inclusive education in her classroom to make inclusion a successful teaching encounter.

References

Dandapani, S. (2002), Value attainment and self image. *Edutracks* 2(4).6-11.

Khandal, H.K. (2003), Value oriented approach from primary to University Education, *University News*. 41(13).9-11.

NEP (2020) Ministry of Education. www.education.gov.in.24,41.

https://www.allfie.org.uk/definitions/what-is-inclusive-education/

https://inclusionbc.org/our-resources/what-is-inclusive-education/

https://www.indiatoday.in/education-today/news/story/nep-s-objective-is-inclusive-education-pm-s-principal-secretary-1924922-2022-03-13

https://www.opensocietyfoundations.org/explainers/value-inclusive-education

https://resilienteducator.com/classroom-resources/inclusive-education/

http://schools.aglasem.com.ncert

https://www.unicef.org/education/inclusive-education

17

Inclusion in Education
A Step towards Social Equity

Rumita Arora (Dr.)*

Inclusion is not tolerance
It is unquestioned acceptance.

Introduction

Inclusion refers to the practice of providing equal access to opportunities and resources for people who might otherwise be excluded or marginalised. In the context of education, it refers to integrating children with diverse needs into mainstream schools. It is in fact much more than the mere enrolment of children with special needs and mental health concerns in regular classroom. It acknowledges the fact that a child's academic potential cannot be developed separately from her/his social enrolment and physical potential, as these are a significant part of a child's development.

Role of School

School years are critical years in a child's development and the school environment plays a pivotal role in shaping a child's growth and outcomes. Yet, three fourths of children with disabilities at the age of five years and one-fourth between 5-19 years do not go to any educational institution. Unfortunately, children with disabilities are overrepresented in the population of children who are out of school and not in the education system. A sound system of inclusion involves creating school policy, building staff capacity and creating a culture that makes it possible for every student to learn. It is absolutely imperative that schools recruit special education counsellors and occupational therapists to support children with disabilities.

Inclusion and Mainstreaming

One way to distinguish inclusion from the other non-segregationist approach called mainstreaming is that in an inclusive classroom, there is a strong emphasis on trying to meet the diverse learning needs of all students without removing

* Assistant Professor, DAV College of Education for Women, Amritsar

them from the classroom. When children with special needs are mainstreamed, it usually means that everyone in the class is expected to follow one standard curriculum regardless of their difference, or that particular children are takenout of the class for a large proportion of the day to receive their lessons and services.

Equity and Inclusion

Inclusion is sometimes thought of restructuring of whole school and class environment in such a way that they are accessible not only to students with impairments but to those who face exclusion on account of culture gender, religion or any other attribute. Inclusion is, in fact, endorsed as a means of achieving a more comprehensive form of social justice. Lots have been said and heard on theories of democracy. There is no denying the fact that contemporary societies withhold the fact that all human beings have equal worth and should have equal rights including the right of access to education. In order to ensure truly universal access to education, principle of equity must be followed. This equity is best achieved by designing an educational system in which physical and social environment curricula, teaching methods recognise and support student's diverse capabilities and needs. Inclusive education is an outgrowth of several social and political movements that have emerged since the middle of the 20th century. It is absolutely essential that we recognise how our own habits restrict equity and social justice and then to find ways to overcome these constraints. Standards of social justice, equity and inclusion are not unique to education. Almost every profession has its own set of rules or guidelines by which members of the profession measure their conduct and performance. We need to prepare social justice educational leaders who advocate and actively engage in promoting inclusive schooling practices for students with disabilities and other students excluded and marginalised. Effective educational leaders strive for equity of educational opportunity and culturally responsive practices to promote each students academic success and well-being. Thus, ushering in social equity and justice replies overcoming silence about all aspects of race, ethos, city, social class, marginalisation and exclusion to make certain we produce schools that are socially just and equitable. In 1990, Individuals with Disabilities Education Act (IDEA) was forwarded. This had three implications: (a) Insistence that communities be responsible for educating children in their neighbourhood schools rather than segregating them; (b) Educate children in the "least restrictive environment"; (c) Individualised assessment of children.

There is a major increase in the number of children diagnosed with disabilities, specifically neurological and psychiatric disorders. Teachers want to create environments in which all students can accomplish their best learning. The foremost challenge is always to meet the learning, social and developmental needs of all students including those with special needs and impairments. We need to create a culture of inclusion wherein many different practices and elements get together in mutually synergistic ways.

Effective inclusion is possible with the help of strong administrative leader who has the ability to change the approach of all stakeholders and make it open minded. In such a set-up, teachers are open to finding creative ways of helping a child function in the class.

Many a time if the class is going on a field trip, teachers and parents can prepare the child beforehand, explaining what to expect rehearsing what the class will be doing. For example, during a music performance, the teachers may ask the relative of a very young child diagnosed with sensory integration dysfunction to be there. A visually impaired student may be permitted to go to the front of the room to read what is written.

Planning of Inclusive Education

There is extensive literature offering guidelines on how lessons and activities can be designed so that they provide multiple ways for students with disabilities, different learning styles to access the material and to show what they have learned. Such "universal design" denotes techniques that help make academic and social aspects of school accessible to all learners. The concept of "different instruction" highlights the importance of what is taught, how it is taught to individual students, learning styles and differences. Inclusive educational practices realise the existence of differences, including ability differences. Inclusive education is about making impairments less central to the way a child is viewed by others, as well as the way he/she sees himself/herself. Inclusion education has much to do with influencing the sense of self and relationship of students. It is important to note that such children should not be made dependent on others. In fact the potential of such children has to be maximised. Of course at the same time, the teachers need to understand how to balance needs of those who require extra attention and resources against the needs of typically developing children. Each child is equally important and none should suffer in terms of time, attention or resources at the cost of another. Also for inclusive education to be viable, teachers and schools need to be given sufficient financial and material resources, training and other forms of support.

Education, it is said, fosters equity and social justice. When it is delivered through a national system which is genuinely inclusive in nature, one that welcomes difference and diversity, then the rights of children become even more secure. It is important to analyse the factors that cause exclusion — "Sharing the blame" for failure. Exclusion can be based on many factors e.g. migration, refugee status, conflict, natural disaster, income, linguistic/cultural status etc.

Diversity lives in each of us. Equality is giving everyone the same pair of shoes. Equity is giving everyone a pair of shoes that fits. When it comes to better understanding of diversity, equity and inclusion, a widened perspective starts with this simple truth. Diversity lives in each of us. Each of us have unique factors that make up and influence our individuality creating a deep understanding of what constitutes diversity, allows us to effectively engage, connect and serve all members of our community.

Conclusion

Every school/class has diversities and the teachers have been trained to manage diversities but within a limited range. Inclusion is a process of addressing and responding to the diversity of needs of all children, youth and adults through increasing participation in learning, cultures and communities and reducing and eliminating exclusion within and from education. This involves modifications in content, approaches and strategies with a common vision and a conviction that it is the responsibility of the regular system to educate all children thus ensuring equity and equality. It is desirable that children learning in inclusive education system should be able not only to develop themselves to their fullest potential but they also play a useful role in local and national economic, social and political development leading to a more just, equitable and cohesive society.

References

https://www.adb.org/publications/strengthening-inclusive-education
https://dir.org/10.1007/s10833-005-1298-4
https:// link.springer.com/article/10.1007/S12564-019-09598-w
https://ummeed.org/inclusion-in-education/
https://users/india/downloads/Kirscher-inclusive-education:sageEncycofCIMgmt2015.pdf

18

Inclusive Education — An Initiative towards Equality, Uniformity and Oneness of Mankind

Sandeep Sharma (Dr.)*

Introduction

If God has created all in his own image and all are equal then we should give equal opportunities to all. Everything in this universe like Earth, Sun, Moon, Planets, Solar System and Galaxies, all are uniform and symmetrical in nature; likewise all human beings are one. There should be oneness and togetherness in all the human beings. All have right to live with equality and uniformity. All have only one life to live; no one can be deprived of their rights and opportunities. One should not be identified from his caste, colour, creed or any inborn disorders; rather everyone should be analysed from their deeds, qualities and virtues. Special children have inborn disorders or disabilities, whatever they are provided with by the will of God. If they have any disorder, they may have some extra qualities too. They are human being like all others, so, equal opportunities for them are required. We must include them with us; in playing, in studies, in every sphere of life. This earth, this universe is common for all. All have equal rights. Especially on education all have equal rights. So, irrespective of all other things, just consider them equal and competent and feel a sense of oneness with them. The sense of this equality and uniformity can be initiated from their childhood, from their kindergarten schooling and so on. For this noble purpose they must be included not excluded in studies and all. So, there is a practical need of the "Inclusive Education". It will surely be an initiative towards Equality, Uniformity and Oneness of mankind.

Inclusive Education — A New Definition and Broader Approach

Initially inclusive education was meant for differently abled children. Later on mentally retarded and children belonging to socially and economically disadvantaged sections were also included into the inclusive education. All these inclusions have been done for quality and complete education for all.

---

*Assistant Professor, PG Department of Chemistry, SMDRSD College, Pathankot

Just including different categories of the learners is not sufficient to fulfill the dream of inclusive education rather different qualities of the teachers and various new methodology of teaching should also be included in this mission. We should include different type of modern teaching methodology into the inclusive education to make the learning easy, better and interesting. We must also include teaching with new modern techniques in the definition of inclusive education. The following should be the definition of inclusive education:

> *"The education system which includes all the children irrespective of caste, colour, creed, group and disability, in the same classroom in the same school, including the modern teaching methodology in the curriculum."*

We are mostly thinking of including every type of children in the inclusive education and thinking that goal of inclusive education is achieved. However, until or unless we do not include all the new techniques and methodologies in teaching, the word "*Inclusive*" will not be complete. So, let us include all the modern technology in the inclusive education, such as:

1. Providing smart classrooms for easy teaching and learning.
2. e-teaching to save the time in paper-pen work.
3. Paperless teaching to save the environment and trees.
4. Online teaching with time and place no bar.
5. 3-D teaching for better understanding.
6. Establishing e-libraries for easy access.

In addition to these, teachers must also include all those honest ways and methods, what we used to talk as our moral duties, a sincere approach for the future making of all the children with whole hearted responsibility. By excluding the 'shirking aptitude' and by including the 'working aptitude' we can really make the dream of 'Inclusive Education' true for all. So, let us include all the includable things for the betterment of our students, our society and the whole world.

Discrimination in the Ancient Times — Need to Learn a Lesson From

Right from the Satya Yuga (Age of truth) to Kali Y*u*ga (Age of vice and misery) there were discriminations on the basis of caste, creed and birth. If we talk about Treta Yuga (Yuga of lord Rama) there was a revered Vedic sage known as Ashtavakra ji; he was having eight bends in his body. He was born a disabled child with eight physical handicaps. He had to face mockery from others but with his wisdom and intellect he proved himself to be superior to all others.

In Dwapara Yuga (Yuga of Lord Krishna) there was Eklavya a son of poor hunter; belonged to an excluded group of people. He wanted to learn archery to save deers from leopards in the forests. He went to Dronacharya for the same but he refused to teach him because Dronacharya was the teacher of only Royal families. Nevertheless, Eklavya made a statue of Dronacharya and accepted him as his teacher. Over the years with his sincerity and self-practice he ultimately became equivalent to Arjuna in archery. This is the extraordinary example of self-study. Nevertheless, Dronacharya demanded to cut Eklavya's thumb as Eklavya had learnt without Dronacharya's consent. The utmost discrimination it was.

Likewise Karana in *Mahabharta* was discriminated on the basis that he is a suta putra (a person born to suta caste parents) i.e. neither kshatriya nor Brahmin. That was also a category of excluded people. On the basis of his caste, no one was accepting to teach him. However, with his determination he completed his education and became a world renowned warrior and philanthropist. So, there were many examples in the ancient times where discrimination on the basis of caste, birth and in-born disabilities etc. could be seen. However, this should not be repeated again, we should learn a lesson from them.

Disability does not Debar anyone from Achieving the Goals

Stephen Hawking was a legendary physicist and cosmologist. At the age of 21 he was suffering from motor neuron disease — a disease that affected the motor neurons in the brain and spinal cord, which gradually paralysed him. Nevertheless, this ailment could not stop him from his research journey. He started his research on black holes and origin of the universe. His IQ (intelligent quotient) was believed to be 160; which falls in the genius category. At the time of his death, at the age of 76, he was Director of Research in the University of Cambridge (England). He kept on with his research work even after his paralysis. He was unable to speak without the aid of computer. He was an utmost inspiration for the disabled persons. He was a live example to all the disabled persons that a physical disability could not stop you from achieving your goals.

Oscar Leonard Carl Pistorius (Blade Runner) lost his two legs when he was 11 months old. He was the 10th athlete to compete at both the Paralympic Games and Olympic Games. He was the first double-leg amputee participant. He was the first amputee to win non-disabled work track medal at the 2012 Summer Olympics.

Many blind and other physically disabled persons have turned out to be very good musicians, composers and music directors. Their sincere practice has made them capable enough. Many disabled persons have qualified civil and other high ranked services. Tom Whittaker was the first and there are a total 15 disabled persons to reach the top of the Everest.

So, everyone has potential and no one can be discriminated on the basis of his/her disabilities. Sometimes, disabilities may give rise to new abilities, which are never even thought of. Hence, everybody should work hard with enthusiasm for achieving their goals in life irrespective of any disability or discomfort.

Paralympics — An Eye Opening Platform

Paralympics are held immediately after the Olympic Games. There are Summer and Winter Paralympics. There are several categories in which the athletes can compete. The allowable disabilities are categorised into ten types. The categories are impaired muscle power, limb deficiency, leg length difference, short stature, vision impairment and intellectual impairment etc. Even these categories are further subdivided into various categories. Special Olympics World Games include athletes with intellectual disabilities and the Deaflympics include deaf athletes. In a nutshell despite various disabilities and problems, para sportsmen and sportswomen play active role in these games and win medals across the globe. So, they are not less than others. Despite their disabilities, they are capable of doing many things. Now, just imagine, if they had been given equal opportunities like other normal students in their school time, college time and university level, the outcome would have been different and more refined too. That is why "Inclusive Education" is given more emphasis nowadays, so that no one should be left behind in availing the opportunities in their life. It is our utmost duty to provide equal opportunities to all the students, rest it is up to the individuals that how much benefit they can have from these.

Perspective of National Education Policy 2020

The National Education Policy (NEP) 2020 envisages equitable and inclusive education for all, with special focus on children and youth, especially girls, from socially and economically disadvantaged groups who are more at risk of being left behind.

The main aim of NEP 2020 is to ensure that no child should lose any opportunity to learn and excel because of the circumstances of birth or background. There are many provisions for making education more inclusive under NEP 2020:

1. Equity and Inclusion
2. Inclusion of Community Participation
3. Gender Equality and Inclusion
4. Inclusion of Skill Courses
5. Inclusion of new Pedagogical System for Early Child Care Education
6. Inclusion of Research at Graduation Level and Exclusion of M.Phil.

The NEP 2020 seeks to ensure inclusive and equitable quality education and hence promote lifelong opportunities for all by 2030. As per recent reports in India there are total 12,99,902 schools out of which only 2,74,445 schools are adhered to inclusive education for disabled children, the proportion is very less, just 21.11%. That is why some strong and firm steps are needed to be taken for this purpose as per this NEP 2020. This is the right time to start the inclusive education properly otherwise further delay will be harmful as we are already very late in this regards. Stitch in time saves nine is the best methodology.

Rights of Persons with Disability (RPWD) Act, 2016

In India, the Disability Act, 1995 has provision of 3% reservation for disabled persons in Government jobs and education institutions. However, after India signed and ratified the United Nation Convention on Rights of Persons with Disability (UNCRPD) in the year 2007, the process of framing a new legislation replacing PWD Act, 1995 began in 2010 to make it in accordance with UNCRPD. It provided that, "the Government will ensure that the PWD enjoy the right to equality, life with dignity and respect for his or her own integrity equally with others, the Government is to take steps to utilise the capacity of the PWD by providing suitable environment." The principle reflects a paradigm shift in thinking about disability from a social welfare concern to a human rights issue.

In RPWD Act, 2016, the list has been expanded from seven conditions to 21. Now it also includes dwarfism, muscular dystrophy, acid attack victims, hard of hearing, speech and language disability, specific learning disabilities, etc. and many more. Persons with Benchmark Disabilities may be defined as those with at least 40% of any of the above disability. All the government and government aided institutions of higher education are required to reserve at least 5% seats for such benchmark disabilities.

So, the government is all set for equality and quality education for all. It would be a paradigm change in the times to come in the education as per the NEP 2020. So, the time has come for scaling the new horizon in inclusive and quality education for all.

Inclusive Education — Need of the Hour

It is the education only which can change the world; the paradigm change. Education is said to be the "Third Eye" of a person. Initially all the human beings are same but once they get eye of knowledge, wisdom and skills they become great and unique. A doctor has the third eye to diagnose ailment of the patients. A doctor also has two eyes like others but still he is capable of seeing the ailment in the patients because of his third eye of medical studies. An advocate has the third eye to analyse the case and to find out the savior solution, an engineer has his own third eye of his knowledge to construct a model initially in his imaginations and then on the ground. Likewise, most importantly a teacher has a third eye empowered by his own subject; the subject in which the particular teacher has done his masters. He is capable of providing the similar type of third eye to his students. Those students are then capable of providing the same to others too. This is the chain reaction by which we can provide the divine third eye of knowledge to the whole mankind. So, by providing the education and right knowledge we can change the mentality of people and hence the whole world.

Education is being imparted but quality education is not. These days the standard of education has fallen down. This can be understood from the fact that graduates and even postgraduates do not know much about their own subjects.

Even many teachers have been seen not knowing their own subjects properly; they are unable to teach their subject without taking book in their classes. If teachers are unable to deliver their own subject lectures to the students then how those students will learn and write orally in their exams. Let's include all these features into our teaching methodology and provide a precise knowledge to all the students. Our students are the future of our country; all of us try to prepare quality students by providing them quality education. Education is that weapon by which we can win the war of successful life. More precisely, not only education but inclusive education is the need of the hour, so that no one should be left behind from this blessing.

Conclusion

It is very much true that we have been given the message of oneness, togetherness, equality, universal brotherhood etc. by all the intellectuals, scholars, prophets, saints and sages right from the ancient time till date. It is also the bitter truth that ever since, discrimination on the basis of cast, colour, creed, birth etc. is continuing. It is a big satire that we are followers of our scriptures, prophets, saints and sages but we do not follow what they have told to us. We are their followers without following them. So, it is an opportunity for us in this era that we should try to follow the path of equality and togetherness with honesty and enthusiasm. Let us start equality, togetherness, oneness in our education system for all the students irrespective of anything else. Education is for all. The paradigm transformation is possible with the help of true education only. Let us pledge for equality and quality education through 'Inclusive Education'.

References

The Rights of Persons with Disabilities Act, 2016, Gazette of India (Extra-Ordinary); 28 December. 2016. http://www.disabilityaffairs.gov.in/uploaad/uploadfiles/files/RPWD/ACT/2016.pdf

The Persons with Disabilities; Equal Opportunities, Protection of Rights and Full Participation; Act, 1995. http://www.disabilityaffairs.gov.in/upload/uploadfiles/files/PWD_Act.pdf

https://www.ncbi.nlm.nih.gov/pmc/articles/PMC5419007

https://en.wikipedia.org

19

Importance of Inclusive Education
Present Scenario in India

Sharanjit Kaur (Dr.)*

Introduction

In present times, Inclusive Education is gaining prominence in education system. The purpose of inclusive education is to integrate children having special needs with the regular class. It includes both the disabled as well as the non-disabled children. One of the main key characteristics of inclusive education is to appreciate individual differences and distinctive set of strengths and weaknesses of each individual. Every child grows into an adult who is completely different from themselves, they have to learn how to establish relations with them and also work with them. This is an important practice as it will result in developing healthy inter-personal relationships later on. A school will be considered to be inclusive if it provides an impeccable ground which trains each child to function appropriately in real life. Here, the children will interact with kids having special needs.

At its core, inclusive education is about appreciating each individual's differences and distinctive set of strengths and weaknesses of each individual. It is not only a philosophical approach towards education but also an important life skill. Children make their transition into a world where they grow up to be adults and have to adjust with people who are completely different from them; learning how to work and develop relations with them is a vital triumph of childhood. An inclusive school provides a perfect platform for training children in preparing them for real life, because daily social, physical and academic interaction between children who are typically developing and their special needs means that they have:

- Enhanced sensitivity — Children who develop in such manner will become more sensitive by learning along with children having special needs. This way, they learn to be more patient, sympathetic and empathetic.
- Have enhanced understanding of strengths and weaknesses — Children studying in inclusive schools will understand that each and every individual

*Assistant Professor, P.G. Department of Psychology, Kanya Maha Vidyalaya, Jalandhar

have their unique set of strengths and weaknesses. They will learn how to appreciate these differences and how to work together, so that they achieve some goal.

- Developing more tolerance — students who receive inclusive schooling realise the value of another human being, regardless of the manner in which the other person looks or sounds like.

Meaning of Inclusive Education

According to Loreman and Deppeler (2002), "Inclusive Education means full inclusion of children with diverse abilities in all respect of schooling that other children are able to access and enjoy." In other words, where there is inclusive education, there will be no separate-out classes, in addition, all sort of students will have full membership to regular classrooms where children having any disability will be able to participate in all activities even if these activities need to be amended. The authors were of the opinion that one of the goals of inclusive education should be to accept children having disabilities. For meeting this goal, a change should not only be brought in the structure and functioning of schools, but also a change should be brought in the attitudes, values and belief system of the school staff.

Inclusion requires that the capacity of regular schools should be increased, so that, if there is any diversity, such schools can respond creatively and effectively. It also involves enhancing the skills and capacities of teachers to deal with diverse student population and attain academic proficiencies that expedite the learning of all students in their classroom. Once inclusive schooling is achieved, integration will not be a requirement as nobody will be left out to be integrated.

The IDEA (Individuals with Disabilities Education Act) legislation (1973) wrote into law rights to a free public education for all students irrespective of their differences and disabilities associated with how they learn. Inclusive education is also referred to as "least restrictive environment". The concept of inclusive education involves providing all students with the same opportunities which are offered to the general population.

Before IDEA, several students having special needs were left out. There were instances when students were sent home from school because of their different abilities. They were not provided the accommodations that are given to students in the present times. An inclusive education system, in its true sense, attends to the needs of child as a whole in all areas of school.

Seven Pillars of Support for Inclusive Education

According to Loreman (2007), there are seven pillars of support for inclusive education. These pillars highlight the essential conditions for inclusive education. These pillars are not mutually exclusive and should be considered inter-dependent.

1. Pillar one: Developing positive attitudes — One of the first requirements for inclusive education is to develop positive attitude among teachers. It has been found that the decisions made by the educators regarding the activities to be introduced to the students should be determined by their attitudes. Therefore, it is very important that educators should develop positive attitude in themselves. In a study conducted by Forlin et al. (1999), it was found that negative attitude towards inclusive education is correlated with low expectations for the achievement of children with disabilities which result in deteriorated student performance. Hence, it is important that school management should take measures to ensure that teachers working in the school should hold positive attitudes towards children having disabilities and inclusive education. This can be attained through devising policies which allow hiring only those teachers who have positive attitudes towards inclusion.
2. Pillar two: Supportive policy and leadership — In order to support inclusive education, there should be policies devised to ensure the creation of inclusive schools. It has been found that even though there are policies which are consistent with the international standards, desirable outcomes are not obtained. The main reasons for this can be that the local educators are not willing to comply with the demands of imparting inclusive education. One of the ways in producing successful outcomes is that the support of the school and system leaders should be procured to create inclusive schools.
3. Pillar three: School and classroom processes grounded in research-based practice — For schools to be effective, it is important that the schools modify and adapt in order to meet the various needs of the learners. A number of organisational factors should be considered at the school level. There should be innovation in scheduling of time and facilities (Jorgensen, 1998). It is viewed that students might not learn at their best in 50-minute lecture, and moving from one classroom to another, taught by various teachers, is a practice which also needs to be assessed. There is need that the educators should consider to have a common planning time. In addition, the students should be divided into heterogeneous groups which will be beneficial in terms of mentoring, social skills and academics
4. Pillar four: Flexible curriculum and pedagogy — It has been found that the curriculum used in various countries is such which leads to teacher-centered instructions. Inclusion will lead to more of student-centered mode of instructions and also in de-centered learning which takes place when one is in small group. Hence, there should be a reformed curriculum which is broader in scope and incorporates the various needs of students with disabilities.
5. Pillar five: Community involvement — One of the important elements in the success of inclusive education is that there should be involvement of

communities in the schools. Greater connection between community and schools shall result in more social cohesiveness and connection. Parents are a significant part of the school community along with the teachers and students. According to Loreman et al. (2005), the roles of the parents can be put into three categories viz. decision-makers, teachers and advocates. The schools should also engage with local, national and international organisations which can cater to the needs of the students.

6. Pillar six: Meaningful reflection — In order to improve one's knowledge and teaching strategies, the teachers should develop a habit of reflecting upon their skills and abilities. Their practice of teaching should be research-based.
7. Pillar seven: Necessary training and resources — It has been felt by the teachers they do not have the requisite training to meet the demands of inclusive classrooms. Therefore, it becomes necessary that appropriate training should be given to the teachers relevant to their educational context which addresses their need. The schools should be adequately resourced in order to meet the demands of inclusive education. The use of technology should also be done judiciously in this case.

Importance of Inclusive Education

It is now understood that one of the goals of an inclusive education system is to include all children. Therefore, it is imperative to understand its benefits for students, teaching staff and the whole school. If we want that all the students should be at par with each other, then it becomes very important that students with disabilities be given the same opportunities as given to others. Students who receive inclusive education should be provided academic, societal, emotional, and physical support. The importance of receiving inclusive education is that when the students make their transition from school to colleges, universities or workplace, they should have an understanding of the significance of co-operation and team-work with people of different types. The development of this understanding among the learners is the building block of inclusive education. It has been found that when students who have disabilities are taught in segregated classrooms, their peers do not always accept them. Hence, the importance of inclusive education is to promote and enhance more teamwork among students and create lesser divisions among them.

Inclusive Education in India

In India, Right to Education Act (RTE) was developed in 2010 which supported inclusive education. This policy focused on both the children having some types of disabilities and other disadvantaged groups (Kalyanpur, 2008). According to this Act, children between the ages of 6 and 14 years should be given free and compulsory education. The policy postulates that children should receive education in elementary school. In addition to this, 25% of the seats in private schools should be reserved for children belonging to lower economic status and children belonging scheduled caste or scheduled tribe (Centre for Civil Society, 2013). Before a child completes elementary school, they cannot be expelled or required to qualify astandardised board exam. Practical suggestions are also provided by the RTE for schools, for example reformed texts and barrier-free environments (Kalyanpur, 2008). It can be said that the progression of policies on inclusive education has been a slow but steady progression. However, there are a plethora of challenges to inclusion such as diverse population and size of India. There are multiple barriers as a result of which students with special needs are being affected in terms of inclusion in India. The schools are lacking the directions of policies on the goals of education. There is not much flexibility in the curriculum and teaching practices, which needs to be modified. Also, there are children who are not able to have access to school education. Hence, this inclusion is made complicated by these multiple challenges.

Conclusion

It is now evident that through inclusive education, the goal of making education universal can be met, various inhibitions and shortcomings can be broken down and eliminated through inclusion, and will lead to an improved education system. In this, teachers have a crucial role to perform as they have the responsibility to provide conducive education. Parents should also be more conscious and vigilant about it.

References

Forlin, C., Tait, K., Carroll, A. & Jobling, A. (1999). Teacher education for diversity. *Queensland Journal of Educational Research, 5.*

Jorgensen, C. (1998). *Restructuring high schools for all students: Taking inclusion to the next level.* Baltimore: Paul H. Brookes.

Kalyanpur, M. (2008), Equality, quality and quantity: challenges in inclusive education policy and service provision in India. *International Journal of InclusiveEducation,* 12 (3), 243-262.

Loreman, T. (2007). Seven pillars of support for inclusive education: Moving from "Why?" to "How?". *International Journal of Whole Schooling, 3(2)*, 22-38.

Loreman, T., & Deppeler, J. (2002). Working towards full inclusion in education. *Access: The National Issues Journal for People with a Disability, 3(6)*, 5-8.

Loreman, T., Deppeler, J. & Harvey, D. (2005). *Inclusive Education: A practical guide to supporting diversity in the classroom.* Sydney: Allen & Unwin.

20

Inclusive Education – Need and Elements

Gurkirpal Singh (Dr.)*

Introduction

Inclusive education entails a major transformation in the existing educational system, from viewing diversity as a problem to appreciating it and giving all necessary assistance to ensure equitable participation.

Current Scenario

In India presently, we have different schools for children of economically weaker section of the society, special schools for meritorious students, special schools for hearing impaired, visually impaired, for mental derangement special facility schools, in which specially trained faculty are present to attend to special needs of differently abled students. For example, visually impaired students are trained in Braille lippie, so faculty having proficiency in Braille are present there to attend to special needs of students. Similarly, students who are hearing impaired, attend schools where they are being given education with the help of sign language, also their teachers are well versed in sign language delivery. Special books are available for visually impaired, similarly, sign language training books are provided to hearing impaired students. Also for mental rehabilitation different teaching schedules are adopted by teachers and trainers for education and betterment of students. All these activities are done in isolation and not under one roof, presently the visually impaired student attends blind school and not conventional regular school, there is a kind of academic exclusion. Present National Education Policy 2020 aims to address these exclusions, aiming at an inclusive society, inclusive education, and acceptance of differently abled individuals or different economic status in mainstream. Inclusive educational systems improve the quality of education for all children and help to change discriminatory attitudes. Schools provide a setting for a child's initial interactions with the world outside of their families, allowing for the formation of social bonds and interactions.

Key Principles of Inclusive Education

All pupils in the same classrooms and schools are referred to as inclusive education. It means meaningful learning chances for previously marginalized

*Assisstant Professor, I K G Punjab Technical University, Jalandhar

populations, such as children with impairments and speakers of minority languages. Inclusive education is based on following seven principles.

1. Diversity strengthens and enriches all communities.
2. Society values, respects, and celebrates all learners' various learning styles and achievements.
3. By taking into account individual requirements and needs, all learners are able to reach their full potential.
4. Throughout the learning process, support is promised and fully resourced.
5. All students require friendship and support from peers their age.
6. In their local communities, all children and young people are educated on an equitable basis.
7. Both within and outside of mainstream education, segregated provision is incompatible with inclusive education.

Inclusive Education - National Education Policy 2020

The National Education Policy (NEP) 2020 aims to provide an equitable and inclusive education for all children and youth, particularly females, from socially and economically disadvantaged backgrounds. The NEP 2020 focuses on delivering equitable and inclusive education, particularly for those who are socially and economically disadvantaged. By 2030, the NEP 2020 aims to "provide inclusive and equitable quality education and encourage opportunities for lifelong learning for everyone". This idealistic ambition stands in stark contrast to India's persistently dismal educational performance. It has brought the issue of inclusive and equitable education to the forefront. The National Education Policy 2020 calls for the creation of a Gender Inclusion Fund (GIF) to strengthen the country's ability to provide equitable, high-quality education to all females and transgender pupils.

The "Gender Inclusion Fund" was included in the National Education Policy 2020 to emphasise the development of girl children. The Government of India will establish a "Gender Inclusion Fund" to ensure that all girls receive a quality and fair education.

The government's strategic approach for the education of all students with special educational needs is defined under the Inclusive Education Policy. NEP 2020 suggests that the Indian government establish a 'Fund' to strengthen the country's capacity to provide equitable and high-quality education to all girls and transgender children.

Elements that Make Up Inclusive Education

Teachers, families, school personnel, inclusive students, other students, supportive special education programmes, and instructional adjustments are among these components.

Best Practices for Building an Inclusive Classroom: Forget about one-size-fits-all teaching methods. All students learn differently, whether they have a disability or not. Create a sense of community, collaborate as a group, and regulate classroom behaviour.

Inclusive education benefits other students: It allows pupils to work on personal goals while interacting with peers their own age. It encourages parents to participate in their children's education as well as the activities of their local schools. It promotes a sense of belonging and respect.

Structured Examination for Analysing Learning (Safal): On the first anniversary of National Education Policy 2020, the Central Board of Secondary Education (CBSE) announced SAFAL (Structured Examination For Analysing Learning), a competency-based assessment for grades 3, 5, and 8.

SEDG in Education: SEDG stands for socio-economically disadvantaged groups, which includes Dalits, other caste groups, and Muslims.

Disadvantage of Inclusive Education

Students and teachers are not psychologically prepared to study alongside people with disabilities. Furthermore, there is the issue of parents' negative attitudes toward their healthy children studying with children who have particular difficulties.

Models of Inclusive Education

Concept, purpose, content, instructional activities, material and learning resource, measurement and assessment method are all included in the model. Co-learning in regular courses of students from various classes, ages, and abilities to serve the many features of students is known as multilevel inclusive education.

Inclusive Education Process

Inclusive education is a method of improving the educational system's ability to reach out to all students. It entails changing school culture, regulations, and procedures so that they can respond to the diversity of kids in the area.

Accepting, respecting, and attending to student differences and diversity, which might include physical, cognitive, academic, social, and emotional factors, is key to a successful inclusive education.

Qualities of a Good Teacher in an Inclusive Setting

- Creating a positive learning environment.
- To accommodate all learners, appropriate teaching approaches and strategies are used.
- Using a wide range of educational resources.
- Students' responses are reinforced.

Benefits of Inclusive Education

Friendship skills, peer models, problem-solving skills, good self-image, and respect for others are some of the advantages of inclusion for children with (or without) impairments. This can also spread to their families, teaching parents and family members to be more accepting of differences.

Deterrents to Inclusive Education

Inappropriate Attitude. Physical Obstacles Curriculum is inappropriate. Untrained educators Insufficient funding. The educational system is poorly organised. Policies act as a roadblock.

Inclusive Classroom

The word "inclusive classroom" is used in pedagogy to describe a classroom in which all students are welcomed holistically, regardless of their talents or skills. It is based on the idea that being in a non-segregated classroom will better prepare special-needs pupils for the future.

Inclusive classroom strategies: Inclusive classroom strategies include following

- Fostering a positive classroom climate
- Learn about your students and let them learn about you.
- Make a safe environment for students to share.
- Provide instruction in a variety of formats/methods
- Select appropriate literature.
- Invite guests to share their personal stories.

Inclusive classroom environment: Every youngster is protected psychologically in inclusive classrooms. Children can explore and develop the opinions, feelings, and ideas that make them who they are in this environment. For being themselves, your child will not be mocked, embarrassed, reprimanded, or rejected.

Conclusion

There are various hurdles and obstacles in the educational system that make it difficult to promote inclusive education. It is not difficult to achieve success in inclusive education in the country with effective tactics and other ways, but there are some issues and challenges that we must address with care.

To ensure that all programmes, including elementary, secondary, and higher education, include adequate teacher preparation, understanding and attitude toward disabilities, and retention of exceptional children, among other things. To ensure the success of the inclusive education programme, more high-quality resources, faculty, and facilities must be provided to each school.

The time has come to establish a unified framework for inclusive education that can serve as a benchmark for participation, access, and inclusion in Indian education, as well as a planning, collaboration, and implementation tool for policymakers. This shared understanding must be formed in collaboration with all key stakeholders, and the goal will be the same as it has been in previous years: to leave no kid behind.

References

Sarkar, T., "Examining disability inclusion in India's new National Education Policy", https://www.ukfiet.org/2020/examining-disability-inclusion-in-indias-new-national-education-policy/

"Handbook-inclusive-education", http://cbseacademic.nic.in/web_material/Manuals/handbook-inclusive-education.pdf, as accessed on 2 May 2022

"Inclusive education", UNISEF, https://www.unicef.org/education/inclusive-education, as accessed on 2 May 2022

Ministry of Human Resource Development, Government of India. 2020. The National Education Policy (NEP) 2020. New Delhi: Government of India. https://www.education.gov.in/sites/upload_files/mhrd/files/NEP_Final_English_0.pdf

UNESCO. 2019. N for Nose: State of the Education Report for India 2019: Children with Disabilities. New Delhi: UNESCO. https://en.unesco.org/news/n-nose-state-educationreport-india-2019-children-disabilities

21

Effectiveness in Inclusive Education
Role of Teachers

Avneet Kaur (Dr.)*

Introduction

The UNESCO Policy Guidelines on Inclusion in Education (2009) states that an inclusive education system can only be created if ordinary schools become more open and accepting; in other words, if schools become better at educating all the children who live in their communities. For some, inclusive education is solely about ensuring that students with disabilities have the same educational opportunities as their peers. However, in much recent literature, 'inclusion' takes on a broader meaning, which suggests that barriers to inclusive education must be considered at any point in time when the participation of students is restricted. Issues may arise for students as a result of a wide variety of reasons including disability, gender, behaviour, poverty, culture and refugee status (Shaddock, Smyth King & Giorcelli, 2007).

The success of every educational programme depends on the quality of the teachers and their attitudes. Implementation of an inclusive curriculum would require a number of changes in the present day teaching practices, curriculum content, evaluation procedures and available resources at the school level without which the goal of providing quality of education would remain elusive. It is also important to mobilise support from parents, the community and special schools.

All over the world, there is now a growing trend to move away from the special schools model to an 'inclusive education'. Inclusive education system views that if a child is not learning, the problem lies in the education system and not in the disabled child. The difficulties arise because of rigid methods and curriculum, inaccessible environment, untrained teachers and poor quality of teaching, lack of proper attitudes on the part of the teachers, lack of support from public agencies etc. thus, the focus shifts from making the education system responsible (Bhargava & Bhargava, 2005). The abilities of children vary, some learn fast while some are slow understanding things. The understanding

*Assistant Professor, Khalsa College of Education, G.T. Road, Amritsar

of various subjects also varies from student to student. Some children can understand the concept of mathematics much faster than their counterparts while other may be good in language skills (Bala & Rao, 2006).

The teacher's role is not only to teach the subject but also to provide other training such as mobility training, self-care training, preparation of teaching material according to the needs of the disabled children, training in use and maintenance of aids and so on. Teaching strategies in respect of specific disabilities have been indicated (Sharma, 2006). It is often argued that a lack of knowledge on the part of classroom teachers, attribute to a lack of training, is the main barriers to inclusion. Inclusion involves the use of support, the ways in which teachers respond to individual differences during whole class teaching, the choices they make about group work and they utilise specialist knowledge (Florian, 2008).

Role of Teachers and Required Competencies in Inclusive Education

Teachers play the most important role in making inclusive education a success. They are responsible for the identification of the children with disabilities in the classroom, referring the identified to the experts for further examination and treatment, accepting the children with disabilities, developing positive attitude between normal and disabled children, placing the children in the classroom in proper places so that they feel comfortable and are benefited by the classroom interaction, removing architectural barriers wherever possible so that children with disabilities move independently. The detailed role of teachers identified in inclusive education is discussed as below:

(i) ***Knowledge of Inclusive Education and Disabling Conditions***
In the context of inclusive education, teacher is required to possess knowledge and understanding of basic terminology and concepts used in special education, a rationale and history of inclusive education, various disabling conditions, policies, programmes and legislations related to inclusive education, rights, roles and responsibilities of parents, students, teachers and other professionals as they relate to individuals with special learning needs.

(ii) ***Curriculum Modification to Meet Special Education Needs***
The teachers teaching in inclusive classrooms are required to modify their curricula to meet the needs of their special education students. The modifications include the provision of an audio-taped text, shortened assignments and summarised chapters of the textbook as well as tools such as graphic organisers and colour-coded chapters to enhance a student's level of comprehension.

(iii) ***Communication with Peers and Head of the Institution***
It is important for inclusive education teachers to advocate the needs of their special education students by ensuring that resources such as peer

tutoring, instructional assistants, team teaching and staff development opportunities are available along with consistent policies that assess the individual student's progress. Teachers also should communicate regularly with the principal to make sure that she is aware of the specific learning needs of the special education students and the academic resources that are necessary for them to experience success in the inclusive classroom setting.

(iv) ***Managing Classroom***

Classroom management for inclusive education includes the knowledge of basic classroom management theories, methods and techniques for students with different learning needs, research-based best practices for effective management of teaching and learning, use of appropriate teaching aids and creating positive atmosphere in the classroom. For example, differently abled students, particularly those identified with emotional and behaviour disorder (EBD) and autism spectrum disorder (ASD), may present unique behavioural challenges for these teachers. The psycho-social environment and also the physical aspects of classroom such as sitting arrangement, lighting and temperature etc. exert a great influence on the inclusive classroom environment. The teacher should adjust and adapt the physical and psycho-social arrangement of the classroom according to the needs of the differently abled children.

(v) ***Managing Positive Behaviour among Students***

Although inclusive classrooms can promote positive peer interactions for special education students, behavioural issues can arise that may require a different disciplinary approach than that used with mainstream students. Teachers may need to consider a developmentally appropriate method for managing the behaviour of their special-needs students. Common approaches often include a system that allows a student to self-regulate and manage his own behaviour, coupled with a reward system that reinforces the student's positive behaviours.

(vi) ***Collaboration among Educational Partners***

Collaboration is the process of merging the knowledge, experience and skills of all partners to meet common goals. Collaboration in inclusive environment is between instructional resource teachers and classroom/ subject teachers in order to carry out problem solving around programme planning, choice of instructional strategies, interpretation of assessment data to inform instruction, participation on service delivery teams, programme planning teams, preparation and/or follow up regarding parent-teacher conferences, sharing resources. Friend and Cook (2010) point out that collaboration between regular school teachers, parents of differently abled students and other school staff is one of the most significant issue in the education of differently abled students in regular school settings.

(vii) Instructional Techniques

This skill is at the heart of all the competencies that regular teachers need to exhibit while working with diverse student population. These skills are the ones that they should use on a daily basis to provide appropriate instruction to special-needs students. A number of specific instructional techniques that regular classroom teachers would require to be competent in include differentiated instruction, activity-based and peer tutoring, experiential learning and collaborative learning.

a) *Differentiated Instruction*: To successfully accommodate differently abled students, regular school teachers needed to practise differentiated instruction. This method requires the teachers to teach one main lesson for all students with variations for each individual student's needs. Thus, a diverse group of learners share an instructional activity in which individually appropriate learning outcomes happen in the same curriculum area.
b) *Activity-based and Experiential Learning*: Using a lecture format as the central form of instruction creates difficulty for differently abled students who are included in regular education classrooms as many students do not learn, retain and apply knowledge as effectively and efficiently. These students require the teachers to deliver instruction that is activity-based and facilitates learning of students through personal experiences. With the use of both activity-based and experiential learning, students become involved in discovery, movement, interaction with the environment and manipulation of materials.
c) *Peer Tutoring*: Peer tutoring is an instructional strategy that involves student partnerships, involving high achieving students with lower achieving students or those with comparable achievement, for organising study sessions. Peer tutoring is believed to minimise behavioural problems.
d) *Cooperative Learning*: Cooperative learning encourages students to work together to complete tasks and solve various problems. Here the teachers need to specify each student's role for the task, clarify the sequence of activities and monitor and evaluate the interactions between the group members.
e) *Individualised and Adaptive Instruction*: Individualised and adaptive instructions are educational approaches that recognise, anticipate and programme for variation according to the student's background knowledge, learning styles, motivation and personal interest. A conceptual framework for instructional adaptations for students with disabilities was provided by Glaser (1977). These adaptations, therefore, require teachers to implement alternative teaching actions such as modifying assignments, materials, testing procedures,

grading criteria and varying presentation styles in order to improve the achievement of differently abled students in regular education classrooms.

(viii) ***Integration of Technology:***

Recent progresses in technology for special needs students has made it possible to accomplish a number of tasks, while being in regular education environment, which was not possible earlier. It is imperative that regular classroom teachers must have at least some level of knowledge and understanding in the use of such devices and software applications (Dimmitt et al., 2006). Apart from the traditional knowledge and skill domains, regular school teachers are now also expected to demonstrate ability in a number of emerging competencies.

(ix) ***Assessment and Evaluation:***

Teachers are required to exhibit efficiency in assessment in order to recognise the specific needs of differently abled students. The teacher has to employ both, basic skills such as gathering, learning and background information of differently abled students and also highly specialised skills such as selecting, administering, scoring and interpreting standardised measurement instruments. Shukla & Singh (2011) suggested that a flexible and implementable scheme of Continuous and Comprehensive Evaluation (CCE) assumes evaluation as a routine activity and exercise of teaching-learning process and it includes all aspects of pupil's growth such as intellectual, physical, personal- qualities, social, interests, attitudes and values through using a variety of tools and techniques by a teacher. CCE is a most suitable procedure due to its fundamental principles of flexibility, functionality, accountability and economy in evaluating a child with disability in an inclusive setting.

(x) ***Professional Development:***

Inclusion teachers should attend in-service training or professional development sessions to hone their skills in curriculum modification, instructional techniques and collaborative teaching strategies that allow special education teachers, specialists and main stream teachers to team teach. Teachers can be benefited by the approach of inclusive education in various ways. It helps teachers appreciate and understand the diversity of individual human being, recognise that all students have strengths and potential, creates a realisation of the significance of direct individualised instruction, enhances ways of creatively addressing challenges. It develops collaborative problem solving skills and skills related to teamwork. It enhances accountability skills and overcomes monotony.

Conclusion

Inclusive education aims at fulfilling the learning needs of special and disabled children who are subject to being isolated and are excluded. The accomplishment of same is being done by providing equal opportunities for all children to participate, learn and have equal treatment irrespective of their physical and mental disabilities. The role of teachers is very crucial in making inclusion a success. Having appropriate professional knowledge about inclusion, understanding of suitable instructional techniques, unbiasedness, capability and willingness to work as a team, collaborate wherever required, using appropriate evaluation techniques to check progress of differently abled students etc. are the important roles of an inclusive school teacher. If mainstreaming is done with a zeal to provide equal opportunities to all needy and all the stakeholders work cooperatively, inclusive can be made a real success. It is rightly remarked, "Children who learn together, learn to live together".

References

Bala, J.M. & Rao, D.B. (2006). *Methods of Teaching Exceptional Children.* Agra: H. P. Bhargava Book House.

Bhargava, M. & Bhargava, R. (2005). *Perspectives of Education.* Agra: H. P. Bhargava Book House.

Dimmitt, S., Hodapp, J., Judas, C., Munn, C., & Rachow, C. (2006). Iowa text reader project impacts student achievement. *Closing the Gap, 24*(6), 12-13.

Essays, UK. (November 2013). Teachers role in inclusive education Essay. Retrieved from https://www.uniassignment.com/essay-samples/education/teachers-role-in-inclusive-education-education-essay.php?cref=1

Florian, L. (2008). Special or Inclusive Education: Future Trends. *British Journal of Special Education, 4*, 202-208.

Friend, M. & Cook, L. (2010). *Interactions: Collaboration skills for school professionals* (6th edition). Pearson: New Jersey.

Glaser, R. (1977). *Adaptive Education: Individual diversity and learning.* New York: Holt, Rinehart & Winston.

McManis, L.D. (2017). Inclusive Education: What It Means, Proven Strategies, and a Case Study. Retrieved from https://education.cu-portland.edu/blog/classroom-resources/inclusiveeducation/

Shaddock, A., Smyth K.B., & Giorcelli, L. (2007). Project to improve the learning outcomes of students with disabilities in the early, middle and post compulsory years of schooling. Canberra, ACT: Australian Government Department of Education, Employment and Workplace Relations.

Sharma, R.A. (2006). *Fundamentals of Special Education References.* Meerut: Lall Book Depot.

Shukla, N. & Singh, V.K. (2011). Inclusive education for children with intellectual disability: challenges and issues. Published in the proceedings of the National Seminar on Mental Retardation organised by Ramakrishna Mission Vivekanand University, Coimbatore, pp.11-18.

UNESCO (2009). Inclusive education: The way of the future. Final Report of the International Conference of Education (48th Session). Paris: UNESCO. Retrieved from: http://unesdoc.unesco.org/images/0018/001829/182999e.pdf.

22

Inclusive Education
Changing Role and Responsibilities of Teachers

Rama Kumari*

Introduction

Inclusive education has been defined at various ways that addresses the learning needs of the differently disabled children. The efforts of the Government of India over the last five decades have been towards providing comprehensive range of services towards education of children with different disabilities. In 1974, the centrally sponsored scheme for Integrated Education for Disabled Children (IEDC) was introduced to provide equal opportunities to children with disabilities in common schools and facilitate their retention. The Government of India initiatives in the field of inclusive education can be traced back to National Educational Policy, 1986, which suggested, as a goal, to integrate the disabled persons with the general community at all levels as equal partners, to prepare them for growth and to enable them to face life with courage and full of confidence. The World Declaration on Education for All adopted in 1990 gave further boost to the different ways of processes already set in the country. The Rehabilitation Council of India Act 1992 initiated a training programme for the development of professionals to respond to the special needs of students with disabilities.

The National Policy for Persons with Disability 2006, which clarifies the framework, civil society and private sector must operate in order to ensure a dignified life for people with disability and support for their families. Most recent advancement is the Right of Children for Free and Compulsory Education (2009) which ensures right to free and compulsory education to all children between ages six to fourteen. For education for a child with any disability, the Act has to be read in conjunction with Chapter V of the Persons with Disability Act, 1995. Chapter V of the PWD Act ensures that every child with any disability is entitled to a free education up to the age of 18 years. Keeping this in view, Government of India had accelerated the new scheme of Inclusive Education to

* Assistant Professor, Department of Education, S.M.D.R.S.D College of Education, Pathankot

achieve the aim of Education for All (EFA) by 2010. Inclusive Education accepts that all children irrespective of their strengths and weaknesses will be part of the mainstream education. Education policy in India has gradually increased the focus on children with special needs in regular schools has become a primary policy objective. In almost every country, inclusive education has emerged as one of the most the important issues in the education system. With the release of the Salamanca Statement in 1994 (UNESCO), many developing countries started reformulating their policies to promote the inclusive education system for students with disabilities into common education classroom. All school going children, whether they are disabled or not, have the right to education as they are the future citizens of our country. Today it is widely accepted that inclusion maximizes the potential of the vast majority of children, ensures their rights, and is the preferred educational approach. In New Education Policy 2020, it was recommended that schemes and policies made for inclusive education are to be implemented to its maximum with an additional support. Inclusive education was another important point raised in National Education Policy 2020, for making physical barrier free education institutions and environment in the country.

According to Dr. S. Radhakrishnan, "Teachers are social Engineers". Teachers are nation builders. Only teachers can understand the needs of the students and improve them by their effective teaching methods of healthy classroom environment. Teachers play an important role in Inclusive Education to facilitate and train all the students for providing the better solutions.

Role of Teachers in Inclusive Education

Inclusive Teacher is a special education teacher who works with inclusion students for better learning outcomes of the students. Inclusive teachers have the following duties —

1. *Classroom environment:* It is important for the teachers to create a healthy environment that allows special needs of students to learn alongside their peer groups. According to teacher's vision, successful inclusive classrooms are those that create a healthy learning environment for a better experience for all the students.
2. *Curriculum design and teaching methodology:* In Inclusive Education, Inclusive teacher helps to craft the curriculum for Inclusive classrooms to ensure that the needs of students with disabilities are considered. Teachers work together to develop curriculum design and new teaching methodology that are accessible to all students.
3. *Collaboration with the regular teacher:* In the general education classroom including inclusive students will have a regular teacher as well as an inclusive teacher. For the effectiveness and achievement of Inclusive

Education objectives both teachers and students are required to work together and discuss the progress of all the students.

4. *Meet individual needs:* Teachers should design educational plans for each student according to their needs, so that they can succeed academically. Teachers know how to accommodate the students and modify works for the students as well.
5. *Cooperative learning:* Another important role of the teacher in Inclusive Education is developing cooperative learning towards the students. This is only possible by setting up tasks and activities to motivate students to learn and experience in groups equally.
6. *Provide facilities and resources:* Teachers have a key role to provide high quality, holistic development and support to the students with the help of resources and facilities according to the needs of the students.
7. *Enabling condition for inclusive education:* The merge of regular and inclusive education will not happen quickly or easily. The process requires regular and inclusive education to consult and collaborate with one another and is plan providing adaptive instructions for all students. From our point of view, the most important enabling conditions are professional training and development of pooling of resources, administrative leadership and support.
8. *Achieving social integration:* Students with disabilities generally do not engage in high level of social interaction with one another unless they are encouraged and supportive in doing so. This lack of interaction among differently abled students includes language and cognitive delays, poor development of play skills and behaviour disorders which include educational needs. It is important for energy and creativity on the part of Inclusive teachers to achieve social integration between students and inclusive education according to the students and develop social interaction with peers.
9. *Skill of Classroom Management:* Physical aspect of the classroom also exerts a great influence on the inclusive classroom environment. Thus a teacher must have knowledge of classroom management methods and techniques for individuals with different learning needs for effective management of teaching and learning process.
10. *Use of Technology:* In inclusive education system, use of technology for special needs students has made it possible earlier. Apart from the traditional knowledge and methodology, regular teachers are now also expected to demonstration ability in the use of technology.
11. *Believing in Students:* A teacher must believe in the student's ability and capability with a clear vision that all the students can learn. In this way teacher will help in removing the barriers and limitations of learning that could marginalise students. The inclusive teacher should recognise

individual difference and motivate to participate in collective teaching because it is essential in implementing education in diversity. The inclusive teacher should have a vast educational view with strong skills, experience and training to participation in inclusive education system.

Challenges to Implement Inclusive Education in India

In India, a large number of the people are disabled, their problems so complex, available resources so scarce and social attitudes so damaging. The aim to achieving inclusive education is a long and varied one, on which challenges and opportunities will arise. Our country is a multilingual, multi-cultural, multi-religious country, and its people are stratified along sharp socio-economic and caste lines. With an estimated 1,210 million people, India is the world's second most populated nation after China. India has 17 per cent of the global population and 20 per cent of the world's out-of-school children. The aim of inclusion is to bring support to all the students. The purpose has become more challenging and difficult as schools accommodate students with increasingly diverse backgrounds and abilities. According to official estimates from the Census of India (Government of India, 2011), the number of people with disabilities in the country is 26 million, or near about 2.1% of the total population. However, UNICEF's Report on the Status of Disability in India (2000) states that there are around 30 million children in India suffering from different disabilities. 10% of the world's population lives with a disability, and 80% of these people with disabilities live in developing countries but 75% of people with disabilities live in rural areas in the India. The government has created numerous policies for special education since the country's independence. There could be many challenges for educating all the children with disabilities in regular classrooms. These challenges could emanate from scarcity of adequate human and material resources, negative attitudes and behaviour of teachers and community, peers and their families. Although the Government has attempted to make policies that are inclusive for children with disabilities, their implementation efforts have not resulted in an inclusive system of education. Moreover, the number of students dropping out from school is getting higher, especially in poverty-stricken areas. Students are forced to leave school due to their families' economic condition, and to work to help their families. This leads to increase the number of child labourers, which in turn leads to cognitive and psychological disabilities. There are particular challenges around negative attitudes and behaviour, on the part of both teachers and family, in relation to the ability of disabled children to learn. Another serious challenge is the fact that most disabled people are still excluded from equal access to mainstream or regular education. Large class sizes present is another challenge for the implementation of inclusive system in the Indian context. Das, Kuyini and Desai (2013) examined the current skill levels of regular primary and secondary school teachers in Delhi, India in order to teach children with differently disabilities in inclusive education settings. They reported that around 70% of the regular school teachers had neither received training and skill in special education nor had any experience teaching students with special needs. Further, 87% of the teachers did not have access to support services in their regular classrooms. According to Sixth All India Educational Survey (NCERT, 1998) about 20 million out of India's 200 million school-aged children (6–14 years) require special needs education in schools. While the national average for gross enrolment in institutions is over 90 per cent, less than five per cent of children with special needs are in schools. Acceptance by peers group provides a much greater challenge for children with disabilities in schools. Children with disabilities are often an easy target for being teased and bullied by their peers.

Conclusion

Education is the fundamental right and to educate all the citizens, teachers have a significant role to play. The disabled students need to be identified, admitted and imparted equality education. The answer is inclusive education. This needs certain skills and competencies on the part of the teachers and therefore professional development and training is essential. Teachers ensure the quality education for all the students in the same Classroom. Teaches with skills, training, educational methodology and support needed to quality education for the students with diverse learning needs with the help of teachers, principal, parents, education officers and policy makers. Regular teachers and inclusive teachers are doing well in collaboration for the achieving of educational objectives. Every teacher has a different experience in inclusive education but communication and having an open mind to suggestions are two key things to keep in mind when working in inclusive education with collaboration teaching.

References

MHRD (2005). Action Plan for Inclusive Education of Children and Youth with Disabilities. Available on http://www.education.nic.in

NCERT (2006). Including Children and Youth with disabilities in Education, a Guide for Practitioners. Department of Education of Groups with Special Needs. New Delhi: National Council of Educational Research and Training. Available on http://ncert.nic.in

Nandini, N., Haseen, Tej. (2014) Inclusive Education: Key Role of teachers for its Success. *International Journal of Information & Futuristic Research*, 1(9).

MHRD (2020) National Education Policy 2020. Govt. of India, New Delhi

National Educational Policy 2020. Retrieved on 08.08. 2020, from https://www.education.gov.in/sites/upload_files/mhrd/files/NEP_Final_English_0.pdf

Prof. N. Pradhan (2020) Teaching competencies for inclusive education. *Journal of All India Association for Educational Research,* Vol. 32, pp. 4-14

www.google.com

www.googlescholor.com

23

Teacher Education for Inclusion

National Perspective

Ruchi Bhargava (Dr.)*

Introduction

Ordinary schools with this inclusive tendency are the most effective means of combating racist attitudes, creating welcoming communities, building an inclusive society and achieving universal education, in addition, providing effective education for the majority of children and improving efficiency and saving costs.

According to Salamanca Statement and Framework for Special Needs Education, 1994, Inclusive Education is a new approach that aims to provide education for students who have been socially, economically and culturally disadvantaged in the general education system. Inclusive education is not limited to children with disabilities, but all children with different backgrounds and abilities (SCERT, 2010). The first amendment to inclusive education at the international level was at the World Conference on Special Needs Education: Accessibility and Quality (Salamanca, Spain, 1994). According to Cobbett and Sleeve, inclusive education is a bold proclamation, a public and political proclamation and a celebration of diversity. It requires a continuous and responsive response to promote a culture of inclusive education.

A comprehensive definition of inclusive education is provided by Johnson (1994), who states that a flexible and independent support system for children and youth with special educational needs (due to disability or other reasons). It forms an integral part of the general education system, and provides ordinary schools that are committed to quality education for all. Such a plan should be considered individually because each learner has different needs. The following statements present a comprehensive view of inclusive education and related thinking.

Inclusive education incorporates a philosophy and teaching process that allows each student to feel respected, confident and secure in order to learn and develop fully. It is based on a set of values and beliefs that focus on the

*Assistant Professor, Khalsa College of Education, Ranjit Avenue, Amritsar

best interests of students, which promote social cohesion, participation, and full participation in learning, holistic school experience, and good interaction with peers and others in the school community. These values and beliefs are shared by schools and communities. Inclusive education is used in school communities that value diversity and promote the well-being and learning quality of each member. Inclusive education is about embracing everything and celebrating diversity. Enrolment is only possible if every child, including children with special needs, has the right to a quality education, with equal opportunities and participation (NCERT, 2013).

Since education is an effective tool for preparing life, or rather education itself is life, it is very important that children be exposed to a wide range of environment in order to cope with life in a positive way. The National Curriculum Framework (NCF, 2005) also suggests that schools should be centres for the health of children and ensure that all children, especially those who are unable to read differently, children from disadvantaged backgrounds, and vulnerable children benefit greatly. Otherwise, they will not be able to cope with the real life challenges they face in different areas of life.

Therefore, integrated education is not only beneficial for children with special needs, but also for other children. Inclusive education is encouraged because it develops social skills and better social interaction because students are exposed to a real environment where they have to interact with other students with different characteristics, interests and abilities. Non-disabled peers develop positive attitudes and actions towards students with disabilities as a result of learning together in an inclusive classroom. Thus, inclusive education forms the basis of an inclusive society that accepts and respects students with diverse skills (SCERT, 2010). The overarching goal of inclusive education is to eradicate all forms of discrimination and to promote social cohesion (SCERT, 2010). It will result in the development of behavioural behaviours for students who may be able to cope with the painful realities of life. Such lasting change will lead to the development of the world.

Inclusive Education in Indian Context

Many policies have been developed to improve education in India since its independence in 1947. As a fundamental right of all citizens, inclusive education was enshrined in the Indian constitution.

Before Amendment, Article 45 of the Constitution states that the State shall strive to provide, within a period of ten years from the commencement of this Constitution, free and compulsory education for all children up to the age of fourteen.

Kothari Commission (1964–66), India's first education commission addressed issues of universal access and participation. A general school system that is open to all children regardless of race, religion, community, economic status and social status has been recommended by the commission. Following the recommendations of the Kothari Commission, the National Education Policy was established in 1968, and the development of an 'integrated system' that allows children with disabilities to attend mainstream schools.

National Education Policy (1986) guarantees equal opportunities for children with disabilities and states that the aim should be to integrate the physically and mentally disabled with the public as equal partners, to prepare for normal growth and to help them cope with life and courage and other minor disabilities will be commonplace with others.

Plan of Action (1992) suggested that special school enrollment should be limited to children whose needs could not be met in mainstream school. After acquiring communication and reading skills, they will be re-enrolled in a regular school. The Integrated Education for Children with Disabilities (Revised 1987, 1989 and 1992) also emphasised that education for children with disabilities should be provided in mainstream schools. A large number of provincial governments have implemented this programme.

Receiving financial support from UNICEF, the National Council for Educational Research and Training in Education (NCERT) used the Project Integrated Education for Disabled (PIED) for the implementation of Integrated Education for Disabled Children (IEDC), launched in 1974 under the Department of Social Justice and Empowerment, (later transferred to the Ministry of Human Resource Development) within the framework of the work and objectives of the National Education Policy.

Department of Special Needs Education was established by the National Council for Educational Research and Training (NCERT) on 1 September 1995 with the aim of educating a variety of talented people in mainstream schools. The department focuses on conducting teacher-training programmes for teachers, educators and policy makers to raise awareness and train them on appropriate strategies to provide quality education and equal educational opportunities for these children in mainstream schools.

District Primary Education (DPEP) programme, which is a national programme, was launched in 1993 with the aim of achieving the integration of primary education (UPE). The main objectives were to reduce the enrollment gap, school dropout and learning success between gender and social groups and to provide all children with access to primary school or equal and informal education.

People with Disabilities Act (Equal Opportunity, Protection of Rights and Full Participation) The 1995 Act of Parliament was passed by Parliament to provide a voice declaring the full participation and equality of persons with disabilities in the Asia-Pacific region.

Later, DPEP was incorporated under the full and integrated programme of the Government of India called Sarva Shiksha Abhiyan in 2001-2002 in an effort to implement Basic Public Education. Its policy was in line with the 86th amendment of the Indian Constitution (2002) which states that Primary Education is a Fundamental Right of every child. One of the main objectives of the SSA was to increase the participation of children with special needs (CWSN) in mainstream education. A number of participatory strategies have been proposed such as promoting enrollment and public awareness to identify school children by emphasising CWSN and promoting the importance of educating these children (SSA, 2005). NCERT National School Curriculum Framework (NCFSE, 2000) recommended inclusive school without specific reference to the student with special educational needs (SEN) as a means of graduating.

The framework of the Inclusive Education Scheme, (MHRD, 2003) also states that inclusiveness is a context in which all students, young people with disabilities or non-disabilities can learn together in standard pre-school, school, and community education settings through the appropriate support service network.

The NCF (National Curriculum Framework) 2005, emphasises that integration policy needs to be applied in all schools and in our entire education system. The participation of all children needs to be ensured in all areas of their lives inside and outside the school. Alternatively, schools should be a life-saving centre and ensure that all children, especially children who are able to function separately from neglected categories, and children in disadvantaged backgrounds benefit greatly critical education (NCF, 2005). Inclusive education has become a major concern for education professionals and policy makers in India.

Role of Teachers in Inclusive Education

1. Critical and Decisive Role: Teachers have a critical role to play in creating inclusive cultural processes in the teaching of the learning environment. The attitudes and values of teachers have a profound and lasting effect on students' self-esteem and self-confidence. All policies and efforts to promote inclusive education will not bear fruit if the people who are responsible for receiving an inclusive education, that is, teachers, lack certain knowledge, skills and values.

2. Educator Must be Aware of, Empathize with and be Motivated: The National Framework for Teacher Education (2009) highlights this fact; it is well-known that a student's level of achievement is determined primarily by the teacher's abilities, sensitivity, and motivation. It is also recognised that the educational and professional standards of teachers are an important part of the learning environment required to achieve educational goals.

3. Teacher with a Variety of Teaching Skills: Preparation of lessons, level and quality of story knowledge, a variety of teacher skills teachers must meet the needs of different learning contexts, level of commitment, sensitivity to class issues and problems as students and level of motivation contribute significantly to high quality curriculum practice. The ideal environment for inclusive education for teachers and educational stakeholders, as well as the other skills mentioned above, should be of great concern.

4. Awareness: It is very important for teachers to have a strong knowledge of the socio-economic background of students. The teacher must not only be equipped to teach but also understand the students and the parent community so that children can stay in school and learn (NCFTE, 2009).

5. Contextual Awareness: Contextual awareness will make the translation process and implementation of the teaching process more effective. Lack of this awareness can create problems that can hinder students' long-term learning. Here the law of readiness will be rejected where non-learning relationships with parents will be helpful to teachers in better understanding students. Awareness of their background will help teachers to communicate with them about different perspectives and understandings. There is no solution for all students. That is why it is said that every student is different and needs to be approached in the right way.

6. Practical Classroom: Classes need to be realistic and reliable in real life knowledge so the curriculum should involve teachers and children in real life rather than just teaching children about theories. It should help them understand the psychological and social aspects and needs of students, their special skills and traits, their preferred methods of awareness, inspiration and learning that come from living at home and in the community (NCFT, 2009). This practice adds student's background information that is useful for scaffolding.

7. Critical and Interpreting Perspective: Teachers need to find interpretive and critical ways of looking at various aspects and knowledge of education and their activities. Teaching knowledge should always be adaptable to meet the needs of different contexts in the teacher's reflection on his/her practice (NCFTE, 2010). Such a view will definitely help them to move forward which will facilitate change of habits.

In line with the policies and recommendations of inclusive education, the curriculum, teaching and learning processes must be restructured in order to achieve the full benefits of inclusive education. It is at this point that the integration of integrated and inclusive education differs. Integration means the physical inclusion of students with disabilities in mainstream schools without change in the school in which students are admitted (SCERT, 2010). On the other hand, inclusive education requires a change in the education system according to the social, economic and children of culturally diverse needs. The National Curriculum Framework (NCF), 2005 emphasises the need for an inclusive curriculum in view of the diversity of learners. It is all about changing the education system (UNESCO, 2005).

In the current context, most teachers find it difficult to identify and respond to the different needs and skills of students in an inspiring and structured way.

Teachers need to recognise that diversity in the classroom as a positive and positive environment for positive change. School administrators and teachers should also realise that, as boys and girls from different socio-cultural and cultural backgrounds and levels of competence learn together, classroom behaviour is improved and motivated (NCF, 2005). The children are gifted with diverse experiences, knowledge, skills and values those can bring some favourable ingredients to the teaching learning process. Teachers need to use a variety of teaching methods, strategies and activities because of the very fact that children's ways of learning are so diverse due to their hereditary factors, previous experience, background knowledge, and environment and personality characteristics. In other words, teachers need to recognise individual differences and implement teaching methods and strategies in such way to fulfill the diverse needs of all learners.

References

United Nations Educational, Scientific and Cultural Organization Ministry of Education and Science, Spain (1994). *Salamanca Statement and Framework for Action on Special Needs Education.* https://www.european-agency.org/sites/default/files/salamanca-statement-and framework.pdf

National Council of Educational Research and Training (2005). *National Curriculum Framework.* https://ncert.nic.in/pdf/nc-framework/nf2005-english.pdf

National Council for Teacher Education (2010). *National Curriculum Framework for Teacher Education.* https://ncte.gov.in/website/PDF/NCFTE_2009.pdf

24

Teacher Education for Inclusion
A European Perspective

Manjinder Kaur (Dr.)* and Navreet Kaur**

Introduction

Highly qualified, subject-specific and dedicated teachers are prerequisites to produce capable human resources (Dogra and Gulati, 2006). Therefore, teacher education in any country always remains an important policy issue (Kumar & Wiseman, 2021). One of the important aspects, which is highly discussed concerning teacher education, especially in European countries, is teacher education for inclusion (EADSNE, 2011). Inclusive education has been defined in different ways; however, all those definitions lead to a common platform which highlights the need and importance of inclusion of all children in the mainstream education system. As per UNESCO (2009), inclusive education may be defined as "a process of strengthening the capacity of the education system to reach out to all Learners and can thus be understood as a key strategy to achieve Education for All (EFA)". As per UNICEF, "Inclusive education means all children in the same classrooms, in the same schools. It means real learning opportunities for groups who have traditionally been excluded – not only children with disabilities but speakers of minority languages too" (UNICEF, 2022). In general, inclusive education may be defined as the education provided to every child under the same conditions irrespective of their physical, mental, social, emotional, economic and cognitive background.

One of the major stakeholders in inclusive education is children with special needs. The concept of inclusive education in the context of special needs children dates back to 1987 when the National Council of Educational Research and Training (NCERT) in collaboration with UNICEF initiated a project titled, "Integrated Education for Disabled Children" (IEDC) (Sharma 2005). The World Conference on Special Needs Education held in Salamanca, Spain in 1994 (UNESCO 1994) gave an active call for inclusivity and solicited nations

* Assistant Professor (Former ICSSR Postdoctoral Fellow), Sri Guru Teg Bahadur College of Education, Khankot, Amritsar

** Assistant Professor, Sri Guru Teg Bahadur College of Education, Khankot, Amritsar

to create and adopt the principle of inclusive education in their education policy frameworks. The advancement of special needs education cannot take place in isolation (Rao, I., 2003) and therefore the children with special needs should be included in regular schools (Kugelmass, 2004) as "inclusion and participation are inherent human rights" (UNESCO, 2009; UNESCO 2021).

Now the question is "who would teach children from diverse (mental, physical, social and economic) backgrounds in an inclusive set-up?" The answer lies in the designing and implementing of teacher training courses and to take other policy initiatives so that a normal teacher with specific training would be able to teach such children in an inclusive set-up. Certainly, specific support measures at the government, school and society levels need to be implemented for an efficient inclusive set-up. This work deals with the concept of teacher education for inclusivity in light of the measures taken by the European Agency for Development of Special Needs Education along with the Module 1 developed by UNICEF for inclusive education (UNICEF 2015).

Methodology

The present work is a subjective appraisal, which highlights the major initiatives taken by the European Agency for Development of Special Needs Education for bringing inclusivity into teacher education. Various published literature reports about the present work have been consulted.

Results and Discussion

Challenges towards Inclusion in Teacher Education in Europe

The schools have to deal with diverse students which increases the complexity of teaching demands to bring and implement inclusion successfully as recognised by the OECD Report (Teacher Matters, 2005). Bringing inclusion while maintaining and developing democratic values, promoting intellectual competencies and social cohesion, combating discrepancies, and maintaining "*sustainable economic prosperity and employability*" are increasingly discussed at the European level, which makes the role of teacher and teacher training very critical. Differences among children are an essential aspect of human development that should be recognised by teachers. The challenges posed by under-achievement in PISA, high dropout rate, migration and mobility and the role of inclusive education in developing a holistic society led to the idea that systematic reforms are needed to develop and sustain inclusive education (Donnelly & Watkins 2011).

Teacher Education for Inclusion (TE4I)

The Council of European Unions at different times set out many requirements for teachers to successfully achieve inclusion (Council of the European Union, 2009). The governments agreed that the trained teachers should be well-qualified and have the skills and competence to support learners. Their understanding of the social and cultural context of education and recognition of the importance of professional development has been recognised to be very important. The European agency for development in special needs education initiated a project named, "*Teacher Education for Inclusion*" (TE4I) in 2007 (TE4I, 2012), wherein 25 countries have participated with a focus on training teachers for bringing inclusion. Initially, descriptive information about teacher education, innovation and the possible ways to enhance inclusion was gathered from participating countries followed by various meetings between country representatives. These meetings along with the study visits to five countries offered enhanced cooperation, networking, and debate on many key issues, especially on the competencies required for inclusive teachers. TE4I project was further supported by an extended Project Advisory Group having members from OECD CERI, UNESCO IBE, EAC, and DG to maintain consistency with other such international and European initiatives (Donnelly & Watkins, 2011).

Outcomes from TE4I

TE4I output includes reports on teacher education for inclusion from participating countries (TE4I, 2012). A 'matrix' document called a project synthesis report has been made, which links evidence from the project directly to the project recommendations. This document extracts information from policy and literature reviews, country reports and study visits and enlists recommendations in the final chapter (TE4I, 2012a). It has been emphasised that the teacher education reforms should be considered societal reforms and the policymakers should consider inclusive education as a key aspect to address marginalisation and exclusion (UNESCO, 2000). Debate and discussion about equity, accountability and standards in education should exist so that the future teachers would be raised in an inclusive set-up with student diversity as equity and school performance move together (Williams, 2006).

The project country reports evidenced different typologies of ways of thinking about inclusion (Ainscow & Kugelmass, 2004) as concerned with: (i) disabled children; (ii) disciplinary exclusion; (iii) all groups being vulnerable to exclusion; (iv) school for all; (v) education for all; and (vi) principled approach towards society and education (EADSNE, 2011). The professional development for the teachers should be developed to ensure lifelong training and steps should be taken to increase the diversity in the teaching fraternity. It has also been stressed that continuous research and follows ups are required to have the most effective approaches toward teacher education. The support measures should be in place to deal with the move from discrete courses of inclusion towards a single course, which prepares all the teachers to cater to the needs of diverse children. Further, the theory-practice gap during teaching practice should be reduced by placing the student-teachers with mentors trained in an inclusive set, who can support inclusion by demonstrating attitudes and values specific to inclusion. Flexible methods should be used for the assessment of teachers both in the institution as well as during teaching practice, for which a strong collaboration between the training institution and schools should exist (EADSNE, 2011).

"*A Profile for Inclusive Teachers,*" (TEI, 2012) is another important output of TE4I, which describes the competencies (knowledge, skills, abilities and understanding, and professional development) of teachers for inclusive education and are not specific to age, phase, country or method of delivery. Each of these competencies has its own listed skills, abilities, attitudes and beliefs along with skills and understanding. Such competencies develop during the Initial Teacher Education and hence are dynamic. Therefore, new approaches to the assessment of competencies should always be devised.

Module 1 for Teacher Education for Inclusion

UNICEF has developed a Module (Module 1) for inclusive education based on the "*Profile for an Inclusive Teacher*" (UNICEF, 2015). The module has five sections where discussions, presentations and activity-based learning is suggested. The module begins with "*Introduction to Inclusion*" which offers teachers to develop a complete understanding of inclusive education and the role as well as the expectation of teachers in making an inclusive set-up. The activity named "*person and system approach*" makes the teachers understand the enablers and barriers towards inclusive education. The sub-section "*Inclusion in Society and Community*" offers an understanding of inclusion at different levels (in society, in community, in school, in the classroom and at policy levels). Such understanding by teachers would help in understanding the real-life situation of a child necessary for bringing inclusion. The information about access, participation and achievement in context with inclusive education at policy (rules and regulations), school (interconnections between teachers, parents and other stakeholders) and classroom level (teacher-child relationship) are also offered.

The second section of the module is related to personal and professional development, which encompasses the teacher competencies for diversity, problem-solving cycle, influences and personal bias, bias in perception, comprehension, reflection, evaluation and projections into the future. The training is based on the model that action not only reflects but affects the attitude and hence affects the teacher's activities. As the intention of a human being is always about problem-solving, thus the model emphasises the same and the teachers need to be first introduced to the problem-solving cycle (Problem-Measuring-Analysing-Planning-Acting-Evaluating). Teachers need to be made aware of the beliefs and biases that can be made at each stage of the problem-solving cycle as per one's understanding, perceptions, intentions and reflections as there is no place for such biases in inclusive education. The module also offers information about the "Professional life-cycle approach trajectory" where teachers need to contemplate their learning as a part of their professional development. The main developmental and professional tasks of a teacher are clarified in this section where novice teachers are trained to leave behind their views about teaching and learning like a student, and the experienced teachers are trained in how to deal with complex situations.

The third section in the module deals with the exploration of social identities, social bias in human relationships and the experience of the effect of social identities by teachers while considering the group of teacher-educators as a social group utilising a questionnaire. After attaining information about social identity, the trainer provides information about the in-group and out-group phenomenon by considering the examples of favouritism, discrimination, over-generalisation of differences between different groups, and minimising the difference between the groups. The learners are informed about how the exclusion takes place with the example of the cycle of oppression affected by prejudice, stereotypes, and discrimination.

The complete understanding of different learning environments by the teachers so that they would be able to support all learners via alterations in learning environments, establish flexible learning situations via linking the present actions with the distant future and practice creative thinking to have out of box ideas to support learners. Participation has been considered a prerequisite to achievement. Thus, the focus is on individual or group activities to develop a deeper understanding of participation in learning by children to promote participation. Similarly, the module also focuses on developing an understanding to create enabling environment via the understanding of appropriate curriculum, support services and procedures to measure student achievement. The last part of the module emphasises working with others (family, community and colleagues) to achieve inclusion, where teacher-educators would be enabled to create a sense of responsibility in the community as well as a family towards inclusion via a set of group meetings, discussions, inquiring about ways to enhance participation and ways that can be used to enhance inclusivity etc.

Conclusion

To have inclusion in general education, it is imperative to bring inclusion into teacher education so that teachers may be trained in such a way that they can teach efficiently in an inclusive set-up. The "Teacher Education for Inclusion" (TE4I) project by the European Agency for Development of Special Needs Education has generated information about trends, similarities, and differences in teacher training programmes in participating countries and identified key issues and challenges for uplifting the teacher education for inclusion. The competencies of teachers for inclusive education have been listed by TE4I irrespective of the age, country and mode of delivery by the teachers. The modules prepared by UNESCO for teacher education for inclusion seem to be developed in a way that the module may be usable in any country throughout the world with minor alterations as per the socio-economic, cultural and other country-specific aspects.

References

Ainscow, M. & Kugelmass, J. (2004). Leadership for inclusion: a comparison of international practices. *J. Res. Special. Edu. Needs*. Vol. 4, (3) pp. 133-141.

Council of the European Union (2009). Council conclusions on a strategic framework for European Cooperation in Education and training. ET 2020. 2941 Meeting of the Education, Youth and Culture Council. Brussels, 12 May 2009. http://www.consilium.europa.eu/uedocs/cms_data/docs/pressdata/en/educ/107622.pdf

Dogra, S. & Gulati, A. (2006). Learning Traditions and Teachers Role: The Indian Perspective. *Educational Research and Reviews*, Vol. 1 (6), pp. 165-169.

Donnelly, V & Watkins, A. (2011). Teacher Education for Inclusion in Europe. *Prospects* Vol. 41, pp. 341–353.

EADSNE (2011). European Agency for Development in Special Needs Education (2011). Teacher Education for Inclusion across Europe — Challenges and Opportunities Ed. Donnelly. V.

Kumar, P. & Wiseman, A.W. (2021). *Teacher Quality and Education Policy in India: Understanding the Relationship Between Teacher Education, Teacher Effectiveness, and Student Outcomes*. Routledge 52 Vanderbilt Avenue, New York, NY 10017.

Rao, I. (2003). "Inclusive education in the Indian context", NCERT, 16-17 September, New Delhi.

Sharma, U. (2005). Integrated Education in India: Challenges and Prospects. *Disability Studies Quarterly*, Winter 2005, Volume 25, No. 1

Teacher Matters (2005). Education and Training Policy: Attracting, Developing and Retaining Effective Teachers. A report by OECD, ISBN-92-64-01802-6 https://www.oecd.org/education/school/34990905.pdf

TE4I (2012). Teacher Education for Inclusion. https://www.european-agency.org/activities/te4i

TE4I (2012a). Teacher Education for Inclusion – Profile of Inclusive Teachers https://www.european-agency.org/resources/publications/teacher-education-inclusion-profile-inclusive-teachers

UNESCO (1994). The Salamanca statement and framework for action on special needs education. http://www.unesco.org/education/pdf/SALAMA_E.PDF

UNESCO (2009) Policy Guidelines on Inclusion in Education. Paris: UNESCO.

UNESCO. (2009 a). Towards Inclusive Education for Children with Disabilities: A Guideline. Bangkok: UNESCO Bangkok.

UNICEF (2015). Inclusive Education: Vision, Theory and Concepts https://www.unicef.org/eca/sites/unicef.org.eca/files/2019-03/ToT_Module%201_0.pdf

UNESCO (2000). The Dakar framework for action: Education for All — Meeting our collective commitments. Paris: UNESCO.

UNESCO (2021). Sub-Education Policy Review Report: Inclusive Education https://en.unesco.org/sites/default/files/inclusive_education_final_-_january_2021.pdf

UNICEF (2022). Inclusive education: Every child has the right to quality education and learning. https://www.unicef.org/education/inclusive-education

Willms, D.J. (2006). Learning divides: Ten Policy Questions about the Performance and Equity of Schools and Schooling Systems. Montreal: UNESCO Institute for Statistics.

25

Creating Space for Diverse Learners

Gurjit Kaur (Dr.)*

Introduction

The diversity of humans' modes of thought and belief, and the variety of customs and worldview along with the rapidly changing population demographics have led to a troubling situation, in which schools and professionals are being challenged as how to provide the best comprehensive educational and support services to their increasingly diverse students population.

The increasing diversity within the schools is demonstrated by the higher visibility of other groups of diverse learners, who differ from one another racially, culturally, linguistically, and socio-economically. The concept of 'Diversity' encompasses more than just ethnic and cultural differences, it includes a wide range of characteristics, viz. gender, linguistic background, socio-economic situation, family life, religion, interests, physical or emotional challenges, skills and abilities and life experiences. The diversity present in all the classrooms provides both challenges and exciting opportunities for instruction to teachers.

To be an effective teacher, one must understand and appreciate human diversity. The classroom in many societies is a representation of pupils with different dimensions of diversity as mentioned above. However, neither does the teacher understand the needs of diverse learners nor s/he can do anything to make learning possible for them.

According to Ginsburg, "Most diversity instruction is geared for abstract sequential learning. We emphasize the development of analytical skills and focus more classes on theoretical and conceptual issues, we eagerly hive "Corrective feedback" and often inadvertently, encourage perfectionism, we rely more on lectures than group discussion and in our small groups we feature the cut and thrust of debate over the exchange of feelings and spiritual insights."

The above observation of Ginsburg seems very true. To succeed in facilitating productive diversification in the classroom, the main principles of productive diversity, full inclusion and accommodation must be diligently applied to course content, materials, assessment criteria and delivery. Since the practice of these diversity principles is tedious, teachers must be convinced of

* Associate Professor, Khalsa College of Education, Amritsar

diversity benefits first. Thus, it is important to promote diversity in teaching and learning to create an inclusive community of critical independent learners. Addressing diversity can also help alleviate anxiety in courses with complex subject matter.

It is noteworthy that rapidly changing demographics demand that we must engage in a vigorous, ongoing and systemic process of professional development to prepare all teachers in the schools to function effectively in a highly diverse environment so that they can deal with diverse learners. Since learning does not take place in vacuum, rather it is based on the transactional relationship between teachers, learners, parents, communities, the immediate and wider cultural and geographical contexts. There are two key challenges to create space for diverse learners. Firstly, the apparent lack of preparedness on the part of teachers and secondly, the lack of attention paid by teachers to the challenges faced by the learners. Contemporary development in educational theory and practice has recognized the necessity to support the needs of a wide range of learners. So, it is the need of the hour that education leaders should move beyond blame and befuddlement and work to transform themselves and their educational institutions to serve well to their diverse learners. The transformative work should proceed in five phases.

Phase I : Creating Environment of Trust
Phase II : Developing Personal Culture
Phase III : Encountering Issues of Social Dominance and Social Justice
Phase IV : Changing Instructional Practices
Phase V : Remodeling the Entire School Community.

Phase I: Creating Environment of Trust

In India, most of the teachers working in schools received their teacher preparation in predominantly teacher training institution which prepare them to deal with average students in regular classes. Thus, many teachers simply have not acquired the experiences and training that would prepare them for dealing with the growing diversity of their students.

The first priority in the Trust Phase should be to acknowledge this challenge in a positive, inclusive and honest way, with focus on; establishing the fact that racial, cultural and economic difference are real and they make a difference in educational outcomes; establishing need for a personal and professional journey toward greater awareness; demonstrating that certain topics can be discussed in an environment that is honest, safe and productive. It can be possible in a climate of constructive collaboration that can be used to address the needs of diverse learners:

Phase II: Developing Personal Culture

Change has to start with teacher before it can realistically begin to take place with students. The central aim of the second phase is to:

- build cultural competence i.e. the ability to form authentic and effective relationship across differences among teachers and diverse learners.
- conceptualize and integrate culture in laying the foundation for the transformation of society and the elimination of oppression and injustice.

Young learners from the marginalized groups or with specific ethnic identity are conscious or sometimes unconscious of the fact that the teachers in their schools really care about them, respect them and enjoy getting to know them as people. It is well known fact that intellectual performance is not fixed and constant quality, but it is quite fragile and can vary greatly depending on the social and interpersonal context of learning. In repeated studies, researchers found that three factors have a major effect on student's motivation and performance:

a) The feeling of belongingness
b) The trust in the people around
c) The belief that teachers value their intellectual competence.

Research suggests that the capacity of teachers in the school to form trusting relationships and supportive learning environments for their students can greatly influence achievement outcomes.

Phase III: Encountering Social Dominance and Social Justice

History of casteism, racism, classism and exclusion in India stare us in the face. System of privilege and preference often create enclaves of exclusivity in schools, in which certain groups are served well while other languish in failure or mediocrity. Demographic gaps become apparent with increasing diversity among learners. While encountering current and historical inequities that affect classroom teaching, the teacher should develop an environment where teachers engage in lively conversation about race, class, gender sexual orientation, and other dimensions of diversity and social dominance. One of the most important functions of the teachers is to transform political jargon like 'Sare Padho Sare Badho' into a moral imperative that inspires teachers to work toward justice, not mere compliance.

Phase IV: Changing Instructional Practices

Students with diverse needs have varying learning styles and schools are expected to adjust for those differences. Traditionally teachers prefer to organize their class in a "logical" order starting with simple premises and working up to a more complex view of the field in question. They use lectures and discussions as the primary means of transmitting information to the students, and classes are usually conducted in a deductive manner.

This phase emphasizes collaborative and interdisciplinary teaching and learning in which students are encouraged to evaluate their own beliefs, understand and compare several interpretations and appreciate that how interpretations are influenced by social identity and background. This means teachers need to examine pedagogy and curriculum; as well as expectations and interaction patterns with students. While dealing with diverse learners, teachers have to promote the following elements of culturally responsive teaching. They should:

- monitor their own behaviour while responding to students.
- allow students need to feel free to voice their opinion and should be empowered to defend it.
- Recognize each student's level of intelligence.
- transact curriculum that honours each student's culture and life experiences.
- encourage students to listen to and value comments made from perspectives other than their own.
- shift instructional strategies to meet the diverse needs of students.

Thus, this phase requires a crucial paradigm shift, in which teachers and other school professionals stop blaming students and their families for gaps in academic achievement. Instead, they may focus on changing their attitudes, beliefs, expectations and practices.

Phase V: Remodeling the Entire School Community

Changing demographics have profound implications for all levels and functions of the school system. To create welcoming and equitable learning environments for diverse learners and their families, teachers must engage the entire community in all the school activities and for the construction of knowledge. The need for direct work with parents and communities have been stressed upon as it increases the relevance of education as well as the quality of learning.

This phase points out that communities provide a context where for the development of concepts in children as well as for the application of school knowledge in real life, that formal knowledge must be linked with community life. The diverse students and community can be conceptualized as a wonderful and exciting element of the world we live in, and not as a hindrance to the educational process. The authentic involvement of parents as active and empowered members of the school community will link school staff with diverse learner, further increasing and affirming cultural diversity within the school settings.

Concluding Remarks

The diversity in classrooms can serve as a catalyst for intellectual or emotional growth, both for the teachers and the students. Seen as an opportunity rather than as a handicap, the diversity of class can facilitate the kinds of change that a school education is designed to promote. In other words, the perspectives that are critical to dealing with the dilemmas of race, culture and language diversity in today's classroom generate intellectual practices such as asking questions, making sense of desperate information, considering and reconsidering precious experiences, gathering and interpreting multiple source of information, appreciating more than one perspective, entertaining alternative solutions and approaches, building on experiential and cultural resources and connecting specific experiences to larger conceptual frames as well as rethinking theories in the light of particular experiences. None of these intellectual activities lead directly to create space for the diverse learners in the classrooms. All of them, however, generate recommendations for curricular, instructional and community practices depending on the school and classroom culture and contexts. This puts on added responsibility on the teacher for which he/she needs to understand the ability of the intellectual and practical work for accommodating the diverse needs of diverse learners.

References

Chandra, Ramesh (2003): *Universal Education and Technology in 21st Century* Vol. II, Kalpaz Publications: New Delhi.

Mishra, R.C. (2009): *Encyclopedia of Educational Psychology* (Vol. III) *Child Psychology*, APH, Publication Corporation: New Delhi.

National Curriculum Framework for Teacher Education Towards Preparing Professional and Humane Teacher (2009): National Council for Teacher Education, New Delhi.

Rastogi, Savita (2000): Training of Teachers in Higher Education for Multicultural Teaching and Learning. *New Frontiers in Education*, xxx, (1), pp. 48-55.

Websites

https://www.reserchgate.net/publication/302396190_chapter_11_creting_space_nd_place_fordiverse_lerners_in_multifarous_contexts.

http://books.google.co.in/books?hl=enandlr=sid=bBpByNijnyw

www.ascd.org/publications/educationl-leadership/mar07/vol64/num06/AS-Diversity-Grows,-So-Must-we.aspx.

26

Challenges and Opportunities to Implement Inclusive Education

In Context of Persons with Disabilities

Suman (Dr.)*

Introduction

The involvement of children with special needs in educational setups has become a primary service decision since the adoption of the UNESCO's Salamanca statement and framework for action of special needs education (UNESCO, 1994). Although inclusion is different in so many means for different people. Thus inclusive education is about participation and achievement of all learners. Inclusive education means including children with disabilities in regular classrooms that have been designed for children without disabilities (Kugelmass, 2004). It is an educational practice based on the social justice that advocates for equal access to educational opportunities for all children regardless of their physical, intellectual emotional or learning disability (Loreman et al, 2005). Inclusive education extends the scope of the school so that it can include a greater diversity of children. Here, society is an inclusive community accepting people of varying abilities/ disabilities, race, language or other attributes. The range of challenges confronting the school system while including children with varied abilities and from diverse backgrounds have to be met by creating child centred pedagogy capable of successfully educating all children. We first have to know about concept of inclusive education and then try to know about various challenges and opportunities for inclusive education of persons with disabilities.

Concept of Inclusive Education

Inclusive education is about safeguarding access to quality education for all students by effectively making sure of their various needs in a system that is

*Assistant Professor, Vaish Arya Shikshan Mahila Mahavidyalaya, Bahadurgarh

responsive, accepting, respectful and supportive. Students contribute in the education program in a mutual learning environment with provision to reduce and remove barriers and difficulties that may lead to exclusion.

Inclusive education is accepted out in a common learning environment; that is, an educational location where students from different backgrounds and with different abilities study together in an inclusive environment. Common learning environments are used for majority of students' regular tutoring hours and may include classrooms, libraries, gym, performance playhouses, music rooms, cafeterias, playgrounds and the local community. A common learning environment is not a place where students with disabilities or other special needs learn in separation from their peers.

Effective Common Learning Environments

- Allow each student to fully participate in the learning environment that is intended for all students and is shared with peers in the select educational setting.
- Provide a positive climate, encourage a sense of belonging and confirm student progress toward suitable personal, social, emotional and academic goals.
- Are approachable to individual learning needs by providing enough levels of support and applying student-centred teaching performs and principles.
- Common learning environment: an inclusive environment where instruction is intended to be brought to students of varied ability and with their peer group in the community school, although being responsive to their individual needs as a learner, and used for the majority of the students' regular teaching hours.

Challenges for Inclusive Education

There are few factors that make implementing and the repetition of inclusive education a challenge for together the government and the people in the country and therefore the disabled children as well. Some of these challenges listed are as under.

1) Parents and Negative Attitudes in Society

Persons need to have good motives and intentions about the practice of inclusive education in both the schools and in society. Slee (2011) writes that people should have a good mindset and encouraging attitude towards inclusive education. As people develop positive attitudes towards inclusive education, applying and practicing inclusive education becomes simple and accessible. In view of that, people need to know the importance of inclusive education. They need to be educated about it and the reasons why they need to grow good behaviour towards disabled children and refer them to regular school to help them get a quality education (Slee, 2011), educating the public will help to embrace and motivate children with disability to be in regular schools.

If successful, these events lead people in the society to admiration and accept disabled children since they see how their families encirclement and accept them to be part of the family and community. When families do not develop good behaviour and attitude towards disabled children, it becomes a challenge for the children to sense as a part of society and, furthermore, people in the community develop a negative attitude towards them (Gadagbui, 2010). When families and the community are educated on the importance of including disabled children within the families, the society and schools, the negative perception formerly developed against them will turn into positive and good behaviour towards the disabled children. In opinion of this, many of them will be lead to school and this will inspire the government in structure more facilities to help their learning and able children as well and creating the necessary organizations in the several schools for disabled children not to feel distinguished from their peers (Ministry of Education, 2015).

In consideration of this, the public and families need to develop good and positive attitude towards disabled children for their inclusion in school which helps with the implementation and practice of inclusive education.

2) Teacher's Negative Attitude

As it comes to families and social attitude towards disabled children, it is important to consider the teachers. For schools to be inclusive, they need to support disabled children and meet the needs of the teachers as well (Hodkinson, 2010). Agbenyega (2007) added that as teachers are trained and become the experience of working with children with special needs, they develop a positive attitude to teach them. However, from study done by Agbenyega (2007) in his conversation, he came across some teachers making complaints about inclusive education. They mentioned that they need provision from principals, authorities and specialists in the schools to help them grip children with disabilities. It is important that they are providing with the expertise to aid them in the schools even though they get the training they need. Moreover, the teachers added that including disabled children in the regular classes affects the academic performance of their peers and the school's academic achievement (Agbenyega, 2007). However, it is important for them to understand that children should learn to develop themselves and that will ultimately help develop the nation.

while discussing with teachers' attitude and providing training for teachers, it will be good and great to discover ideas about facilities that care their training and donate to the important development of a positive attitude towards children with special needs.

3) Lack of Facilities and Infrastructures

If teachers have to develop a positive attitude towards inclusive education, they should first be educated, trained and supported. The government needs to provide the various schools with the resources and support to help with the practice and application of this program. Appropriate facilities and infrastructures need to be provided in the schools to inspire and motivate teachers to teach disabled children (Kuyini, 2010).

Teachers develop a negative attitude to inclusion because of large class-size in several of the schools. In my experience from back home, there were around 40 to 50 students in a classroom and this makes it problematic for teachers to appear to all students, particularly disabled ones. As there are various children in one classroom, it is problematic for the teacher to take care of all and this makes inclusive education a challenge. Therefore, it is vital for the government to provide more facilities to accommodate fewer students in the classroom for teachers to grip all. (Alhassan, 2014). With this in mind, families, society and teachers must develop positive attitudes towards inclusive education. It is important to keep in mind the benefit and possible opportunities inclusive education takes.

Opportunities for Inclusive Education

Allthough there are some challenges of implementing and practicing inclusive education, there are opportunities as well. Educating children with disabilities in the many schools is an gain for everyone (Mihai, 2017). This subdivision will discuss some of these opportunities of inclusive education.

1) Building and Providing Facilities

Inclusive education has several advantages for children with disabilities as well as parents, schools, teachers and society. It leads the government to provide more facilities. As the government wants to implement and practice inclusive education, it shapes more schools and provides more facilities which do not only benefit disabled children but everyone around them.

Furthermore, as the government shapes or provides more facilities, it effectively reduces the cost because it is more economical to shape facilities that accomadate and benefit all children than building distinct facilities for disabled children (ObengAsamoah, 2016). As the government decreases cost by giving facilities to benefit everyone, they can use the remaining money to help train additional teachers and develop expertise to help the teachers grip and teach varied students in the schools (Agbenyega, 2007). As teachers are trained, they become innovative ideas, techniques, teaching approaches and elegances to teach disabled students. This develops teachers to be creative and innovative in their teaching strategies (Gadagbui, 2010). As more facilities are provided and teachers are trained, this encourages the implementation and repetition of inclusive education to become active. This then leads to the provision of suitable teaching aids and equipment to sustenance all children to learn which types children's needs and interests taken care of. Still, it inspires more flexibility in the teaching methods and approaches by teachers (Gadagbui, 2010). This furthermore leads to positive attitude developed by teachers and children. Therefore, inclusive education inspires the government to deliver more facilities and resources towards its implementation and practice.

2) Developing Positive Attitudes

Inclusive education lays both non-disabled and disabled children in the same school and classroom with teaching methods that benefit all of them. The atmosphere is free and safe. There are facilities to accommodate all children and this encourages everyone to develop positive attitudes to disabled children. When teachers are educated, trained, and empowered in inclusive practice, it helps to develop positive attitude and behaviour in the direction of disabled children (Alhassan, 2014).

Furthermore, families and society develops positive attitudes and healthy environment when they have knowledge about inclusive education. It encourages a union between the school and parents, creation teachers and parents help each other in helping disabled children within schools. This inspires parents who want to withdraw their children from schools to reconsider their choices (Gadagbui, 2010). As contended by Slee (2011), everyone should be able to understand the value of inclusive education which principals people to hold and support all children with disabilities in the schools and communities. This encourages people in the communities to help them do their homework as well as extra activities (UNESCO, 1994). As the children are supported and encouraged, it takes them closer to people which helps us all to develop a positive attitude and good behaviour in the direction of them (Agbenyega, 2007) and this enable them to participate in the society as well. Inclusive education ensures people will develop positive attitudes towards disabilities.

3) Developing Themselves and the Society

Developing good behaviour towards children with disabilities inspires them to participate in the school. It helps them to get a appropriate quality education to develop themselves. Inclusive education encourages quality education and social development for disabled children. Furthermore, as disabled children are developing themselves, acceptance, appreciation and admiration from people around them is created and this helps to make tolerance and harmony among people in the country. This helps to develop the country by creating a good future for today's generation and the generations to come and to a superior degree, include everybody whether disabled or not to live with each other in society (Mihai, 2017). It increases social inclusion, builds relations, encourages networking and provides opportunities for people to interact amongst themselves as with other communities and nations (Gadagbui, 2010), thus, preparing all for inclusive life and society in the future. Therefore, it is important to implement inclusive education for disabled children to develop themselves and their country. Everyone's contributions is required in the development of the country.

Conclusion

As mentioned above, there are factors that prevent the inclusion of disabled children into the schools. Moreover, they need to be trained with good teaching methods, strategies, and styles as well as classroom supervision to include all children in their teaching methods. As teachers are trained and supported with inclusion in mind, they develop a positive attitude and good behaviour towards all children which makes inclusive education to be effective. Furthermore, non availability of facilities was another challenge for the implementation and practice of inclusive education. If facilities are not provided to empower and support teachers and the disabled children, it becomes a challenge for both teachers and children. This discourages the parents to send their children to schools and makes some of them droplet outs of the education system.

Despite the challenges, there are similarly great opportunities in the practice of inclusive education. Inclusive education creates various opportunities which include making the government builds or provides additional facilities to benefit concurrently differently abled and nondisabled children, teachers, parents and society in general. Building and providing more facilities inspire more children to attend school and helps avoid children from dropping out. As more facilities are provided, it involves more teachers to be trained and supported. Parents are encouraged to refer their children to schools as they can trust on that facilities are being provided to support their children's learning and safety in the school. Last but not the least; this inspires collaborative work between parents and teachers. As parents support their children to appear in school, society grips them and they get the chance to attain an education in order to develop themselves and so their society.

References

Agbenyega, J. (2007). Examining teachers' concerns and attitudes to inclusive education in Ghana. *International Journal of Wholeschooling*, 3 (1). Retrieved from https://files.eric.ed.gov/fulltext/EJ847471.pdf

Agbenyega, J. & Deku, P. (2011). Building new identities in teacher preparation for inclusive education in Ghana. *Current Issues in Education*, 14(1). Retrieved from http://cie.asu.edu/.

Alhassan, A. M. (2014). Implementation of inclusive education in Ghanaian primary schools: A look at teachers` attitudes. *American Journal of Educational Research*, 2 (3), 142-148. Retrieved from http://pubs.sciepub.com/education/2/3/5/index.html#.

Ametepee K. & Anastasiou, D. (2015). Special and inclusive education in Ghana: Status and progress, challenges and implications. *International Journal of Education Development*, 41, 143-152. Retrieved from https://doi.org/10.1016/j.ijedudev.2015.02.007.

Armstrong, A. C., Armstrong, D., & Spandagou, I. (2010). *Inclusive education: International Policy and Practice*. London: Sage Publication Limited.

Banks, J., A. & Banks, C., A. (2010). *Multicultural Education: Issues and Perspective*. Seventh edition. Hoboken: John Wiley and Sons, Inc.

Gadagbui, G., Y. (2010). Inclusive education in Ghana: Practices, challenges, and the future implications for all Stakeholders. Retrieved from www.schoolsandhealth.org/.../Inclusive% 20Education%20in%20Ghana.pdf.

27

Educating Special Learners
A Challenge

Jaspreet Kaur*

Introduction

There have always been exceptional children but there have not always been special educational services to address their needs. Some individuals in one or more ways are different from normal, average individuals, who account for some of our population, thus making them "special" owing to their different needs. Special education classes provide a unique service to physically or mentally challenged students. The ideal special education classroom provides quality instruction to students with disabilities. While the push in education these days seems to be toward online education and the inclusion of special education students within mainstream classrooms, special education classes are still needed for more severely disabled students. The purpose of the specialized classroom setting is to provide more intensive, individualized attention to the students who most need it. The present article focuses on greater attention to the processes of special education so as to achieve viable results relating to the art of teaching. There is a need for honest rethinking and purposeful action to reorient teaching methods so that measurable outcomes are achieved for educating special learners. Special education seeks to provide specially designed instructions for students with disabilities or who have special learning needs using specially designed materials, teaching techniques and facilities. It also focuses on different types/categories of special learners like visually challenged; academically challenged etc. It further defines its characteristics, manifestations and modified teaching strategies to meet their requirements. In this article we have tried to focus on different categories of exceptional / special learners (challenged learners) and special facilitation strategies for them. Overall, the emphasis is to adopt special teaching strategies so that the quality of life of challenged learners can be improved and they can be helped to develop self-confidence.

Though no two individuals on this earth are similar, there are some individuals who are different from normal individuals in one way or another

* Assistant Professor, Khalsa College of Education, Amritsar

and can be clubbed in a category termed as special because they require special education. This special education which involves special teaching strategies, instructions, facilities and methods is usually fabricated to meet the unusual demands of exceptional / special learners. In this article, we have tried to focus on different categories of exceptional / special learners (challenged learners) and special facilitation strategies for them. To understand them, teachers should design learning strategies specifically for them. They should have knowledge in psychology and also an attitude of empathy and concern towards them. Major emphasis is given on the concept of special education, types of special learners different teaching strategies and role of community and society towards them.

Concept of Special Education

It is an instruction given by professionals to those students who have any disorder or disability. Disorder refers to a general malfunction of mental, physical or psychological process. Disability is more specific than a disorder and results from loss of physical functioning like loss of sight. A 'Handicap' is a limitation imposed upon the individual by the environmental demands and is related to the individual's ability to adjust or adapt to those demands. Such learners have some special needs which must be catered to in the classroom. Such kind of students require modification in regular classroom practices to develop to an optimum level. Such individuals should never be labelled which is an unhealthy practice as they already have poor self-esteem. The contemporary view and practice is to use the term 'challenged' to connote exceptionality or special needs. Way back in 1960's, people with disabilities were integrated into large societies and Principle of Normalization came into force. 'Normalization', a philosophical belief in special education in which every individual, even the most disabled should have living environment as close to normal as possible. As a result of this, two important movements came into action:

1. De-institutionalization
2. Regular Education Initiative (REI)

In De-institutionalization, the trend was to move people with disabilities into closer contact with community and home, thus making a larger society for them. The US Government in 1980 took an initiative of REI which emphasized upon general education. The focus was on educating children with special needs along with mainstreaming which is the practice of placing them in general classes. Later came an era of 'Full Inclusion' in which all students with disabilities were placed in general educational classroom. There are a number of people and institutions who serve such kind of students like.

1 Regular classroom teacher
2. Itinerant teacher (who moves from one institute to another)

3. Resource person
4. Diagnostic centers
5. Residential Schools and colleges.

Types of Special Learners

A learner is considered as special in today's classroom if he is with differential gifts and challenges. He can be categorized on the basis of special needs and nature of challenges he faces. Following are the challenged categories:

1. Autism: Disability with communication and social interaction
2. Visual impairment: Disability in use of vision
3. Hearing impairment: Disability in process of hearing
4. Orthopedically challenged learners: Such kind of learners require special care in functional use of hands, arms, legs and other body parts
5. Academically challenged learners: Disability in terms of intelligence.

1) ***Autism***: It is a developmental disability which affects verbal and non-verbal communication and social interaction with people. Autism has been derived from the Greek word "autos" which means self, which indicates extreme sense of isolation and detachment from the world around them. It is one of the most disruptive childhood disabilities which results in varying degrees of deficiency in language interpersonal skills, and emotional or intellectual functioning. It is caused by damage to Central Nervous System or due to change in genetic factors.

   Manifestations

   - Irregularities and impairment in communication
   - Engagement in repetitive activities
   - Stereotyped movements
   - Resistance to environmental change in daily routine
   - Avoids eye contact
   - Do not respond to physical affection
   - Prefers inanimate objects
   - Impulsive and inconsistent in their responses
   - Low IQ (70 units or less)
   - Difficulty to abstract information
   - Fail to focus on one or more stimuli.

   Teaching Strategies

   - According to the requirements, and needs of individual learner, IEP (Individual Education Programme) is framed.
   - Involvement in social activities, hobby clubs to promote involvement.
   - In the lesson plan, try to break down a difficult problem into a series of non-complicated subtasks.

- Exercise patience and empathy toward them.
- Be supportive to them.
- Work on positive, increasing appropriate behaviour rather than focusing on in appropriate behaviour.
- Counsel for medical intervention in the form of drugs

2) ***Visual Impairment:*** Individuals with such kind of impairment are generally categorized as partially sighted and blind people.

   Partially sighted individuals are able to use their sight in some way to read i.e. by using special glasses. Blind people are unable to read by means of vision, therefore, they have to use their fingers to read Braille. According to medico legal standpoint, a person is considered as blind if the central visual acuity in both eyes is less than 20/200. Individuals with visual acuity ranging from 20/200 to 20/70 are called partially sighted. Visually impaired individuals generally have associated problems like mental retardation, sensory defects, learning disability, and motor defects.

   Manifestations.

   Red rimmed or swollen eyes, inflamed or watery eyes, itching, burning sensation, headaches, double vision, excessive rubbing, blinks more frequently, holds book close to eyes, squints eyelids together.

   Teaching Strategies

   - Teacher can modify the lesson plans in such a way that same instructions can be delivered to all the students including special learners.
   - National Federation of Blind has lobbied for Braille bills to increase its availability and to establish Braille competency for students with visual impairment.
   - Large print books and audio tapes can be used for them.
   - Technological devices can be used.
   - Mobility training which involves the usage of guide dogs, and electronic devices.
   - Stress upon independent living and development of employment skills.

3) ***Auditory Impairment***: Such kind of learners are of two types i.e. Deaf and Hard of hearing.

   Manifestations

   In deaf individuals, auditory channels fail to serve as a means of processing speech. It has been observed that individuals who are deaf and who have parents who are deaf have higher reading achievements than individuals who are deaf, but they have hearing parents. This is due to the fact that deaf parents are able to communicate more easily with deaf children with the help of their sign language. In hard hearing individuals only one auditory channel is working at some level of amplification for receiving speech. This impairment is due to pre- and post-natal infections like rubella, meningitis, genetic disorders and other causes like trauma and toxic substances.

Teaching Strategies

- Educator of deaf student should adopt a blend of oral and manual techniques like "Oralism" and "Manualism".
- They should stress upon speech reading sign system, finger spelling, and auditory verbal approach.
- Use sign language.
- Take help of technological advances like hearing aids, television, telephones, CAI (computer assisted instruction) and information super highway which includes linguistic differentiation.

4) ***Orthopaedically Challenged Individual***

Medically orthopedic impairment can be defined as impairment caused by congenital anomaly, polio, T.B., neurological disorder like cerebral palsy, TBI and musculoskeletal disorders. Individuals with physical disabilities have physical limitations or health problems that interfere with attendance or learning to such an extent that special services, training, equipment, materials or facilities are required.

Teaching Strategies

- Educate them to avoid adolescent pregnancies, as teenage mother can give birth to premature or low birth weight babies.
- A healthy interface between parents, teacher and community is required to provide healthy atmosphere for their personality development.
- Prosthetic (replacing a missing body part) orthodics and Adaptive (Aids a person's daily activity) devices should be used.
- Educational plans should be developed to improve individual's intellectual, sensory physical, and emotional abilities.
- Try to make them independent and sell sufficient.
- Prepare them for advanced education and work.
- Tell them to choose career according to their intellect, emotional and motivational levels.

5) ***Academically Challanged Learners:*** Such kind of learners find difficulty in the mainstream, unless the curriculum and pedagogy is modified for them. They can be categorized as slow learners, under achievers and learning disabled

(A) Slow learners: A slow learner is an individual whose mental ability is high enough to justify keeping him in the regular classroom but low enough to give him considerable difficulty in keeping up with the average speed of the class. His I.Q. ranges in between 70-90, as a border line case. Such kind of learners asks many questions and isolate themselves from their peers because they find them as dull and boring. Practically they are slow in all aspects of development. They verbalize information in a diffused manner and possess poor co-ordination. They lack self-reliance and get poor grades everywhere. In comparison to peer group, they are slower in physical and social development.

Teaching Strategies

- IEP (Individual Education Plan) should be developed by the teacher which is based on complete information of the candidate. Teacher should try to integrate this with all other activities.
- Task analysis should be done in such a manner that subject matter can be subdivided into small number of units so that the learner does not find any difficulty in transferring information from one lesson to another.
- He should accept this fact that the mental insufficiency is not the learner's fault.
- He should lay emphasis on what that individual can do, not upon what he cannot do.
- Use criterion referenced evaluation coupled with innovative teaching methodology.

(B) Underachievers: When a student with a high I.Q. performs poorly i.e. there is a large discrepancy between the child's performance in the teaching institution and his innate ability, he is said to be an underachiever. Similarly, a child whose performance is below average is called an underachiever. Such kind of individuals lack goals and motivation. They have poor study habits and are not interested in work. They fail to complete assignments in time as they do not concentrate. They become aggressive or timid because they are not consistent in their approach.

Teaching Strategies

- They need emotional support – love patience and care.
- Individual attention and counseling should be given so that he verbalizes his feelings and instills a sense of security.
- Create a healthy and conducive classroom atmosphere which does not impose or make excessive demands on the student. Provide him freedom to explore and give space to grow into a confident individual.
- Cognitive restructuring strategies should be used like, count your blessings, thought stopping and negotiations.

(C) Learning disabled: Learning Disability is a general term that refers to a heterogeneous group of disorders manifested by significant difficulties in acquisition and use of listening, speaking, reading, reasoning, or mathematical skills. The disorders are due to CNS dysfunction, genetic factors, poor classroom teaching. Persons with such kind of disability exhibit a great extent of variation from person to person in their psychological and behavioural patterns. They find problems in written or spoken language and mathematics. Such individuals have cognitive problems which lead to disorganization and metacognitive problems and are rejected by their peers.

Practitioners use tests like Standardized achievement tests, Informal reading inventories etc. to assess students with learning disabilities.

Educational Strategies

- Cognitive training should be given.
- Thought process should be changed.
- Self instruction, mnemonic keyboard method and scaffold instruction should be used.
- Behavioural modification is essential e.g.; student's attention should always be rewarded whereas his in attention should never be punished

Conclusion

The author concludes with a few words to parents and teachers who are actually working with learners having disability,"It is all in the mind that matters", hence it is the attitude of family which determines whether it is a stressful or humiliating condition or a challenge which can be overcome with support system. We should adopt various facilitation strategies for special learners to give them extra care, attention, and show great concern in improving their quality of life.

References

Francisco, Marian & Hartman, Maria & Wang, Ye. (2020). Inclusion and Special Education. *Education Sciences*. 10. 238. 10.3390/educsci10090238.

Sharon Vaughn and Sylvia Linan-Thompson, (2003) What Is Special About Special Education for Students with Learning Disabilities? The University of Texas at Austin 140, *The Journal of Special Education* Vol. 37/NO. 3/PP. 140–147

Chall, J.S. (2000). *The academic achievement challenge: What really works in the classroom?* New York: Guilford Press.

Abbott, M., Walton, C., Tapia, Y., & Greenwood, C. R. (1999). Research to practice: A "blueprint" for closing the gap in local schools. *Exceptional Children*, 65, 339–352.

Artilles, A. (1998). The dilemma difference: Enriching the disproportionality discourse with theory and context. *Journal of Special Education*. 32, 25-31.

Bynoe. P.F. (1997. May). Increasing the diversity of the special education teaching force through an innovative recruitment effort Dissertation Abstracts International. 5ti, 05A (University Microfilms No. 97-34051).

Bynoe, P. (1998). Rethinking and retooling teacher preparation to prevent perpetual failure of our children. *Journal of Special Education,* 32J 37-40.

Carnine, D. (1997). Bridging the research to practice gap. *Exceptional Children, 63,* 513-52M

Comer, J. & Woodruff, D. (1999). Everyone counts: Developing schools that work. *Metropolitics* 3(1), 11-15.

Craig, S., Jull, K., Haggart, A.G., & Perez Selles, M. (2000). Promoting Cultural Competence through Teacher Assistance Teams. *Teaching Exceptional Children, 32(3),* 6-12.

Kea, C., & Utley, C. (1998). To teach me is to know me. *Journal of Special Education, 32, 44-47.*

Kromrey, J.D., Bines. C.V. Paul. J., & Rosselli. H. (1996). Creating and using a multi paradigmatic knowledge base for restructuring teacher education in special education: Technical philosophical issues. *Teacher Education and Special Education, 19(2"),* 87-101.

28

Expedition of Inclusion in Education

Bindu Sharma (Dr.)*

Introduction

Article 21A states that the State shall provide free and compulsory education to children between 6-14 years of age. But is it sufficient to provide education to all the children irrespective of its benefits to them? Here the concern should not only be the provision of education to all the children but more important aspect is to make sure either this education is beneficial to all or not. Yes, here the author wants to talk about the education of children with special needs. Before 1700s the education of these students was totally ignored. They were considered as a burden on the society. Neither society nor parents took any initiative for their education. In the mid of 1800s, some of the educationists raised their voice for the education of these deprived children with special needs, but their education was restricted to special schools only and this system of education was known as segregated system of education. As per the Encyclopedia of Special Education, the establishment of special education began in 1832 with the first school for deaf in Kentucky. The trend towards segregated education reached its high point during the 20th century. In India, segregated education of children with disabilities began with the establishment of first special school in Amritsar in 1884 by Anne Sharp, a missionary manager (Mani, 1998; Pandey and Advani, 1997). During 1950s and 1960s, parents' organizations in the USA initiated advocacy action for education of their children with disabilities. A group of special education leaders, such as Blatt, Dunn Cruickshank, Hobbs, Lilly and Wolfersberger began advocating the right of students with disabilities to learn in more normalized school environment with their peers. The Indian Education Commission (1964-66) was the first statutory body to suggest that education of handicapped children has to be organized not merely on humanitarian grounds but also on grounds of reality. In 1986, the National Policy on Education (NPE) was formulated which emphasized that "whenever feasible, the education of children with locomotor handicap and other mild handicap will be common with that of others". In 1987, the Project Integrated Education for the Disable (PIED), was implemented by

*Associate Professor, Khalsa College of Education, Amritsar

Ministry of Human Resource Development, Government of India. The Person with Disability Act (PWD Act) 1995, has made integration of students with disability a legal responsibility of the government. Article 26b endeavours to promote the integration of students with disabilities in the normal school. In the present chapter the author has tried to highlight the journey of education of children with special need from the era of segregation to inclusion.

Historically we have had two educational systems — one for children with disabilities (education in special schools) and one for everyone else (education in regular schools). The movement towards integration of children with disabilities in regular schools started in the second half of the twentieth century. The trend at present is to create one education system that values all children — to devise a classroom that welcomes all children irrespective of disability, community background, sexuality, ethnic background, etc.

Internationally, the drive towards inclusion of children with special needs into mainstream regular school is fueled by a number of initiatives like segregation, integration and inclusion. Before 1700s the education of persons with disabilities was totally ignored. They were considered as a burden on the society. Neither society nor parents took any initiative for their education. Benjamin Rush, a physician in the late 1700s, was one of the first Americans to introduce the idea of educating persons with disabilities. As per the Encyclopedia of Special Education, the establishment of special education began in 1832 with the first school for deaf in Kentucky. At the end of the American War of Independence, a number of philanthropic organizations played a leading role in the establishment of training institutions for people with disabilities. Segregated institutions for individuals with disabilities continued to grow in number and size during late 19th century until the 1950s. This trend towards segregated education reached its highest point during the 20th century.

In India, segregated education of children with disabilities began with the establishment of the first special school in Amritsar in 1887 by Anne Sharp, a missionary manager (Mani, 1988; Mukherjee, 1986; Pandey and Advani, 1997). However, Miles (1997) also reported that the first special school for mentally retarded and physically handicapped children began in India at Kurseong in 1918. The education of children with disabilities continued to be provided in segregated settings following India's independence in 1947. Of course, various NGOs assumed increasing responsibilities for the education of children with different types of disabilities. There were more than 1200 special schools by 1997 (Pandey & Advani, 1997).

Along with establishment of special schools, special classes in public schools were also expended in some cases for education of children with disabilities. "Special classes came about not only on humanitarian grounds, but because such children were unwanted in the regular classroom" (Chaves, 1977). Another notable feature is that special educators were in a regular school, but in many ways were not a part of it. General and special education developed on parallel rather than on converging lines. But during the 1950s and 1960s, the use of special classes in public schools was the preferred education delivery system for most of the students with disabilities. It was during this period that the public attitude about the place of individuals with disabilities in schools and in the community began to change.

The Movement from Segregation towards Integration

During 1950s and 1960s parents' organization in the USA initiated advocacy action for education of their children with disabilities. A group of special education leaders, such as Blatt, Dunn Cruickshank, Hobbs, Lilly and Wolfersberger began advocating the right of students with disabilities to learn in more normalized school environment with their peers. During this period, a large number of special educators were exploring the possibilities of integrating children with disabilities into the regular classroom.

In the early 1970s, various court decisions in the USA established the right of all children labeled as mentally retarded to free and appropriate education. Pressure by parents, courts and legislators resulted in Education for All Handicapped Children Act of 1995 which was enacted in 1978. This law, reauthorized as the individuals With Disabilities Education of 1990, which extended the right to a free public education to all children, regardless of disability, in the least restrictive environment possible. The term 'integration' was thus formally introduced in 1978 (Peter Clough, 2000). By the late 1970s and early 1980s, many disabled students began to be integrated into regular classroom on at least a part time basis. By the 1980s, attempts to educate children with disabilities in the regular classroom on a full-time basis were intensified. Integrated education for disabled children was favoured practice in all countries up to 1994 (World Conference on Special Education Needs at Salamanca, Spain).

A number of international and national initiatives have contributed to the movement towards integrated education in India. The Indian Education Commission (1964-66) was the first statutory body to suggest that "education of handicapped children has to be organized not merely on humanitarian grounds but also on grounds of reality". Integration of children with disabilities into regular classroom could draw the attention of State Government after the Ministry of Welfare, Government of India initiated the scheme of Integrated Education for Disabled Children (IEDC) in 1974. The centrally sponsored scheme of IEDC was revised in 1981 and later in 1992 allowed 100% assistance to state government for implementation of the scheme. Moreover, non-government organizations were also involved in providing education to disabled children in the regular classroom.

The United Nation declared 1981 as the International Year of Disabled Persons. "Full participation with Equality" was the underlying theme of the programme. India's response to the UN's declaration was the development of National Plan of Action to provide comprehensive services including integrated education for persons with disability.

In 1986, the National Policy on Education (NPE) was formulated which emphasized that "whenever feasible, the education of children with locomotor handicap and other mild handicap will be common with that of others". In 1987, the Project Integrated Education for the Disable (PIED), was implemented by Ministry of Human Resource Development, Government of India. In 1992, the Economic and Social Commission for Asia and the Pacific (ESCAP), at its 48th session held in Beijing declared 1993-2002 as the Asian and Pacific Decade for Disabled persons. India attended the ESCAP committee meeting and pledged to implement the recommendations on full participation and equality of people with disabilities. The Person with Disability Act (PwD Act) 1995, has made integration of students with disability a legal responsibility of the government. Article 26b endeavours to promote the integration of students with disabilities in the normal school. The District Primary Education Programme (DPEP), a major internationally assisted prorgramme was launched in the country to reform and renew the primary education system of the country. It was implemented in the selected districts in a phased manner. One significant feature of DPEP is its emphasis on integrated education for the disabled. The remaining districts, which were not covered under DPEP, were covered under Sarva Shiksha Abhiyan (SSA). SSA was launched to achieve the goal of Universalization of Elementary Education. This adopts a zero-rejection policy and uses an approach of converging various schemes and programmes. A zero rejection has been adopted under SSA, which ensures that every child with special needs (CWSN), irrespective of the kind, category and degree of disability, is provided meaningful and quality education. Although the Government of India had made several attempts to integrate the disabled into regular classroom, it lacked in firm commitment to promote integration. In spite of all these policies and acts, integrated education could not succeed and the trend is directed towards inclusive education.

A Worldwide Movement towards Inclusive Education

In education, 'inclusion' refers to the placement and education of children with special need in regular classroom with children of the same age who do not have any disability. The underlying premise of inclusion is that all children can learn and belong to the mainstream of school and community life. Inclusion means full inclusion of children with diverse abilities in all aspects of schooling that other children are able to access and enjoy. It involves 'regular' school and classroom genuinely adapting and changing to meet the needs of all children as well as recognizing and valuing differences among them.

Internationally, the drive towards inclusion of children with special needs into the mainstream of regular school is charged by a number of initiatives and treaties including the UN Convention on the Rights of the Child (1987), the UN Standard Rules on the Equalization of opportunities for person with Disabilities (1993), Jomtien World Declaration on Education for All (1990) and the World Conference on Special Needs Education (1994).

The World Declaration on Education for all, Jomtien, Thailand, which was reaffirmed in the Dakar Framework for Action (2000), gives the message: in order to attract and retain children from marginalized and excluded groups, education system should respond flexibly. Education system must be inclusive, actively seeking out children who are not enrolled, and responding flexibly to the circumstances and needs of all learners. In 1994, representatives of 92 governments and 25 international organizations formed the World Conference on Special Need Education in Salamanca, Spain. They agreed to a new dynamic statement on the education of all disabled children, which called for 'inclusion to be the norm'. The statement calls on the international community to endorse the approach of inclusive schooling and to support the development of special needs education as an integral part of education programmes. In particular, it calls on UNESCO, UNICEF, UNDP and the Word Bank for this endorsement.

Inclusive education which has emerged as a reform in the education of children with special needs gained momentum since 1994 World Conference on Special Needs Education. It is significant that some countries have made significant advances towards promoting inclusive education which includes Canada, Cyprus, Denmark, Iceland, India, Luxembourg, Malta, Netherlands, Norway etc. At the same time, inclusion had been the of heated debate for teacher educators and among special education leaders. There were some fundamental questions needed to be attended in any study on inclusive education. These questions are: What does inclusion imply? What is inclusive education? What does an inclusive classroom look like? How is this inclusive approach different from traditional approach?

Generally, in education, 'inclusion' refers to the placement and education of children with disabilities in regular education classroom with children of same age who do not have disabilities. The underlying premise of inclusion is that all children can learn and belong to the mainstream of school and community life. Inclusion does not mean 'dumping' children with special needs into the regular classroom. We have to accept their diversity, respect their individuality, create opportunities for their participation in all the activities of the school, and provide support to both children and teachers so that children can realize their full potential and teacher will be able to improve their performances. The main goal of inclusion is to ensure that all children, regardless of any individual difference they may have, are fully included in the mainstream of life. But we do not know the time frame when all children will be fully included in the mainstream of school and community.

What does an inclusive school look like? "A school that promotes inclusion is called inclusive school. An inclusive school is a place where everyone belongs, is accepted, and is supported by his or her peers and other members of the school community in the course of having his or her educational needs met" (Stainback, 1990; Stainback & Forest, 1989). Inclusive schooling is the process of operating a classroom or school as a supportive community where the needs of all members are met, and people support and accept responsibilities for each other.

Inclusive approach is different from traditional approach as it is a community-based approach. An inclusive school reflects the community as a whole. Membership of the community is open, positive and diverse; it is not selective, exclusive or rejecting; it is barrier free; an inclusive school is accessible to all who become members — physically in terms of the building and ground, and educationally in terms of curricular support system and methods of communication; it promotes collaboration; an inclusive school works with, rather than competitively against other schools; it promotes equality, an inclusive school is a democracy. (Thomas, Walker, & Webb 1998). By far the most important reason for promoting inclusive education is in terms of its benefits for both children with disability and those without disability, including gifted children.

Benefits of Inclusion for Children with Disabilities

Mc. Gregor, G and Vogelsberg (1998) list the following benefits of inclusion for children with disabilities based on a comprehensive view of research literature:

- Children with disability demonstrate high level of social interaction with non-disabled peers in inclusive settings when compared with segregated settings.
- Social competence and communication skills of children with diverse abilities are improved in inclusive settings. This is believed to be closely associated with greater opportunities for social interaction with non-disabled peers.
- Social acceptance of children with diverse abilities is enhanced by the frequent small- group work nature of their instruction in inclusive classrooms. Children get to see beyond the disability when working in small groups, and begin to realize that they have much in common with children with disabilities.
- Friendship more commonly develops between children with disabilities and those without disabilities in inclusive settings. Researchers have found

that children in inclusive setting have more durable networks of friends than children in segregated settings. This is especially true of children included in their local neighborhood school, where they can more easily see friends outside the school hours.

Other benefits of inclusion for children with disabilities include:

- Inclusion assists in the development of general knowledge for children with disabilities.
- Children with disabilities who are included in regular schools tend to become adults who spend more time in leisure activities outside of the home, spend more time in leisure activities with adults without disabilities, and spend more time in community work setting than do their counterparts educated in segregated settings

Benefits of Inclusion for Children without Disabilities

In many ways children without disabilities are also benefited from inclusion as much as children with diverse abilities. The following benefits of inclusion for children without disabilities have been substantiated in the literature:

- The performance of children without disabilities or giftedness is not compromised by the presence of children with diverse abilities in their classes.
- The perception that children with diverse abilities can disrupt a class is largely unsubstantiated in the research literature.
- Children without disability and giftedness can benefit from improved instructional technology in the classroom. Other children can benefit from the presence of these technologies, and can use them when they are not required by child with diverse abilities.
- Children with disabilities or giftedness can benefit from increased funds in the classroom. Extra funds and resources removed from 'special programmes' can be used in the regular classroom to enhance the learning of both types of children.
- Frequently, extra funding for children with diverse abilities is directed towards the provision of additional staff, either special teachers or para-professionals. In either
- case, the presence of an extra adult in the classroom opens up a wide range of possibilities for all the children.
- Children without disabilities or giftedness involved in peer-tutoring can benefit from improved self-esteem and mastery of academic contents. Furthermore, it has been found that peer tutors demonstrate a higher mastery of academic contents in a given area than do their peers who are not involved as tutors.

- Children without disabilities or giftedness have the opportunity to learn additional skills such as Braille or sign language.
- Children without disabilities or giftedness learn to value and respect children with diverse abilities in inclusive classroom. It will help them to get out of associated social stigmas towards children with disabilities.

Conclusion

In nut a shell we can say that inclusive education is a practice of including everyone — irrespective of talent, disability, socio-economic background, or cultural origin — in supportive mainstream school and classroom where the needs of all students are met. By educating all children together, children with disabilities have the opportunity to prepare for life in the community, teachers improve their professional skills, and society makes the conscious decision to operate according to the social value of equality.

References

Claves, I.M. (1997). Historical overview of special education in the United States. In P. Bates et al. (eds.) *Mainstreaming: Problems, Potentials and Perspectives,* Minneapolis, National support system project.

Mani, C. (1998). *The Physically Handicapped in India*, Ashish Publishing Ltd. New Delhi.

Mc. Gregor, G. and Vogelsberg, R.T. (1998). *Inclusive schooling Practices: Pedagogical and research foundation.* Paul H. Brookes. Baltimore.

Miles, M. (1997). *Disabilities, care and Education in the 19th Century India: some Dates, Places and Documentation* (ERIC document, No. 498747). NCERT, New Delhi.

Mukherjee, S. (1986). The inclusion of pupils with a chronic health condition in mainstream school: What does it mean for teachers? *Educational Research*, 42(1) pp.59-72.

Pandey, M. and Advani, L. (1997). *Perspective in Disability and rehabilitation.* Vikas Publication. New Delhi.

Stainback, S., Stainback, W., and Forest, M. (1989). *Educating All Students in the Mainstream of Regular Education.* Paul Brookes. Baltimore.

29

Social Inclusion of Children with Special Needs in Rural Areas
Problems and Role of Education

Hiranmoyee Medhi*

Introduction

Man is the wonderful as well as beautiful creation of God. At birth, man is quite helpless. He does not have the ability to look after himself like the other animal on earth. He is to be fed, nourished and looked after by his parents, relatives or other members of his family. It is necessary to teach and train children about various things related to their livelihood. They have to adjust with changing environment and live a healthy and peaceful social living.

The environment is not always stable. It is changed day by day or time by time. Therefore every individual should have the sense of adjustment. Children can learn this ability from their parents, ancestors and other society members. They pick up social rules and regulations, do's and don'ts and acquire knowledge and skills to solve different types of problems. To make a socially acceptable individual, the human child gradually develops himself in the society. His behaviour becomes mature as the child is growing in different stages of his life. In social environment, the behaviours are transmitted from one generation to other by means of various rituals, laws, traditions, customs, morals, languages, literatures, ideologies, cultures and other norms and elements of society.

Every individual is born with certain probabilities and personality traits. No one is equal to others. There are individual differences on the basis of different grades or norms. Child's abilities and potentialities are developed when they come in terms of other people. The family members; teachers and class fellows or senior and juniors in educational institutions; relatives; neighbours; and other society members have a great contribution in formation of child's social development. Through interaction, co-operation, conflict and competition, individuals come to contact with others and willingly or unwillingly they learn social behaviour and personality.

---

*Assistant Professor, Department of Education, Deomornoi Degree College, Darrang, Assam

Socialisation of Children

The process of acquisition of knowledge for social adjustment and development of social abilities is simply known as socialisation. As an innocent and unlearned human being, every child learns his first lesson of all his actions in family. After family, gradually from his playmates to other companions, he learns to behave as a socially acceptable individual. As a member of the society he has to obey social rules, regulations, laws and other formalities. He becomes a responsible social member and does his duties for himself, for society and for the nation as well. The entire process of building his socially approved personality may be called socialisation. It is the duty of society to provide sufficient atmosphere so that every individual can exist with his own identity. Society should produce moral support for truth, humanity, co-operation and other values. It should also establish high ideals, such as honesty, tolerance, self-regard, self-sacrifice, love for others, and respect for elders etc. which bring moral values, peace, happiness and aesthetic senses among the society members. It is necessary for individual, social and national development.

Children with Special Needs

Children are the future of every society. Disabled children are also an integral part of the society. The social prosperity relies on all round development of every child. Without the development of disabled children, total development of the society is impossible. In this regard, it is necessary to impart knowledge and training for their better livelihood. They need special care, attention and training. The Right to Education Act, 2009 furnishes a great deal for education and development of these children by implementing free and compulsory elementary education. Inclusive education provides an important role to make people aware of education, needs, problems and facilities available for children with special needs.

The children with special needs basically involve children from gifted or talented, physical disorders, mentally retarded, learning disabled, emotional and behavioural disorders, communication disorders etc. They need some additional services in home, school and social environment, because their needs and problems are very different from the normal children. They have difficulty in adjustment, education and communication. A unique cooperation and support from parents, teachers and society members are utmost important to develop according to their abilities and complexities. As they have a difference from the norm of normal children, so an individualised and psychological programme of education and training will help them in their all-round development.

The gifted and talented children have their superior intellectual power that is manifested in their all activities. Visually impaired, hearing impaired, deaf and dumb, orthopedically handicapped children come into the category of physically handicapped children. Children with low intellectual abilities are mentally retarded. The children have disability in listening, reading, writing, reasoning and arithmetical skills are learning disabled. There are children with difficulty in speech and language, communication and behaviour disorders. Autism is another type of disability found in our society.

Social Inclusion

All creations are precious and have a unique value in their respective environment. Human beings contribute their specific role in society. Each and every individual has a great role in formation, development and progress of their social groups. Each of us has definite abilities, potentialities and characteristic elements to live in the society and help others to live happily and co-operatively.

In every society, individuals should have same and equal opportunities to participate in each and every activity performed in the society. Their abilities and potentialities are expressed and developed in social environment. At the same time, society gives the platform to bloom individual's prosperity. All the functions and elements of society are managed and organised by individuals. So, each and every person without any discrimination has to involve social relationships and organisations.

Social inclusion is the state of including members within a group or structure. It is an act of taking part in every activity of a group. There is no discrimination applicable to all the members where they have been included. Social inclusion means all the members of the society have equal and probable opportunities to participate and co-operate in all socio-cultural activities and enjoy full freedom to perform their equitable role in society. Students have vast amount of probabilities in them. They share their values and status with others. Through social inclusion everyone can live a co-operative and better adjustable life by involving fully and actively in society. Social inclusion reduces social discrimination; empower poor and disadvantaged groups of people; and make all people identical in all social grounds.

The disabled children are also the valuable members of the society. They too contribute their best for social formation, progress and prosperity. There are lot of example of various personalities with disabilities in different grounds, who have not only contributed remarkably to their society, but also to the entire world. Albert Einstein, the creator of the Theory of Relativity, was a person with disability in learning. Stephen Hawking, the genius well-known physicist was diagnosed with a motor neuron disease called Amyotrophic Lateral Sclerosis (ALS) where he lost his speech. George Washington, the first President of United States, had disability in learning named, dyslexia. Helen Keller was a person with hearing and visual impairment. Ludwig Van Beethoven, the famous musician was hearing impaired. The famous motivational speaker Nicholas James Vujicic is with Tetra-Amelia Syndrome, a physical disorder of absence of arms and legs. Multi-talented world personality Walt Disney was a person with dyslexia. Indian famous actress and Bharatanatyam dancer Sudha Chandan and The Mount Everest Mountaineer Arunima Sinha, both are physically handicapped women. The list of famous disabled persons who have contributed contributed to social, cultural, economic, scientific or political grounds is not short. The disabled children can prove that their disability is not strong enough to stop their will power to achieve them into the top position of society.

Advantages of Social Inclusion for Children with Special Needs

For the children with special needs, social inclusion provides the following advantages-

a. Builds confidence to make friendship with other children in the society.
b. Broadens understanding among other members of the society about abilities and problems of disabled persons.
c. Increase tolerance and develop respect in their mind for every member of the society.
d. Teaches responsibilities to obey social rules and regulations and make dutiful for whole society as well as the nation.
e. Normal children learn to value the roles and contributions of disabled children and understand their limitations.
f. Builds positive attitudes such as empathy, acceptance etc. among all members of the society.
g. Helps to build their personality through positive and effective behavioral traits.
h. Strengthen them to avoid their weakness and disabilities.
i. Encourages to maximize their willing power and do something best for their lives and for society.
j. Ensures well being of all the children irrespective their difficulties and minimize discrimination in society.
k. Protects disabled children from abuse, negligence, exploitation and other ill-treatments.
l. Changes attitude towards disabled children and develop awareness for their educational and vocational empowerment.

Problem of Social Inclusion of Children with Special Needs in Rural Area

In rural area, disabled children face various problems in their development due to limitations of all facilities. There are a few numbers of educational institutions where sometimes quality education is become a big dream for common people. There is poor condition of all the facilities including education, nutrition, medical etc. People in rural community still believe that disability is the sin of parents and the result of their bad deeds They become victim to social evils like superstition, social discrimination or narrowness. Maximum people are illiterate and poor socio-economic conditioned to spread awareness on education and development of disabled children.

The major problems of social inclusion of children with special needs in rural areas are-

1. The rural people are not aware of education of disabled children. They think educating disabled children is the wastage of money and effort.
2. The negative attitude among rural community results in various social inequalities and discrimination in gender, caste, class, ethnic origin, religion etc. which hampers to bring these children to participate in social relationship.
3. Due to low literacy among rural areas, people generally believe in traditional prejudices. They do not give equal importance to disabled children with normal children.
4. In rural areas, there are poor conditioned medical services. Disabled children have a lot of physical and mental disturbances. They need frequent health check-up, therapy and counseling services. Due to limited facilities in rural areas, disabled children are deprived from medical treatments whatever they need. As a result, they limit their position to home and cannot join social activities.
5. Most of the parents are not responsible for meeting needs of disabled children and force them to live a better life. Sometimes, the poor parents cannot offer routine meal or afford basic human necessities because of their low income.
6. The public services are not designed friendly to meet the unique needs of disabled children. For that, disabled children cannot participate in social institutions. Hence, to engage them in public institutions is restricted, which makes them excluded from society.
7. Generally, disabled children do not have any friends. In rural areas, parents of normal children do not allow their child to play or make intimacy with disabled. As a result, these children develop inferiority complexes and maladjustment in society.
8. The rural schools have poor infrastructure. There are problems of trained teachers, teaching learning materials, transportation and other recreational facilities. Disabled children cannot reach their unique needs in rural school and gradually they have to leave school and are excluded from society.
9. Poverty is a major cause of social exclusion of disabled children in rural areas. There is lack of parental awareness to bring their disabled children in social upbringing. For poor economic condition, parents do not allow their disabled child to engage in any groups, associations and training courses.
10. In most of the rural areas, the social discipline is sometimes not in balance due to household quarrels, alcoholic addicted people, anti-caste and anti-religious activities. The alcoholic parents have lack of willingness to

participate in social organizations and festivals and unaware to send their children to school. These children are excluded in society because of their parental unfriendly and antisocial behaviors.

Role of Education in Social Inclusion

Education is a process through which children learn to adjust in every social environment. Without social development, man is not fully developed and become a selfish human being. It eradicates social discrimination, poverty, injustice, inequality and other social evils. Education is an essential condition for the society and of the society. The progress of every society is based on progress of its individuals. Education prepares individuals to develop their different qualities; makes a productive human being; and builds their personality to play different role in society.

Education plays the following role in social inclusion of disabled children-

1. Education develops qualities and potentialities of children with special needs to conform to the norms and ideals of their social life.
2. Education grants liberty to disabled children to enjoy certain rights to form his social behavior and develop his personality.
3. Education removes social evils like, superstition, narrowness, discrimination on gender, age, class and caste, harassment, victimization, prejudices etc. It also removes disability discrimination, which help disabled children to do their needful and give chances to share their feelings, workability and contributions in different social grounds.
4. Education gives training on economic self-sufficiency to children with special needs, so that they may become productive member of the society and able to reduce unemployment problem.
5. Education builds awareness among parents, teachers and other members of the society to provide sufficient facilities for total development of disabled children.
6. It ensures understanding, sympathy, cooperation and friendship toward disabled children by other members of society.
7. Education reduces social vulnerability and poverty and improves standard of living of children with special needs by giving them opportunities to do services in different levels.
8. Education develops moral values, integration, love and respect for all human being. It gives chances to disabled children to take part in social activities.

Conclusion

The concept of social inclusion is the key factor for development of a nation. It leads to equality, fraternity, integration and enrichment of all human resources. Children with special needs are like the other members and also the part and parcel of society. A democratic and welfare state cannot develop by leaving them apart from all socio-economic conditions. In rural areas, there are various factors that hampers in social inclusion of its members. Education changes the scenery of social exclusion and brings awareness for total development of children with special needs. It helps them to participate in all social activities.

References

15 Inspirational People with Disabilities. (n.d.). Retrieved from Narayan Seva Sansthan: https://www.narayanseva.org/blog/15-inspirational-people-with-disabilities

Abbott, S., & McConkey, R. (2006). The barriers to social inclusion as perceived by people with intellectual disabilities. *Journal of intellectual disabilities:JOID, 10* (3), 275-287.

Aggrwal, J. C. (1996). *Theory and Principles of Education.* New Delhi: Vikas Publishing House Pvt Ltd.

Chutia, M. K. (2018). *Special Education.* Guwahati: Lawyer's Book Stall.

Das, P., & Talukdar, B. (2016). *Special Education.* Guwahati: Surya Prakash.

Deka, B., Nath, K., & Hussain, R. (2014). *Bishesh Siksha.* Guwahati: Ashok Book Stall.

Mathur, S. S. (2000). *A Sociological Approach to Indian Education.* Agra: Vinod Pustak Mandir.

Pathak, G., & Deka, A. (2016). *Special Education.* Guwahati: Surya Prakash.

Rai, B. C. (1998). *Theory of Education.* Lucknow: Prakashan Kendra.

Samagra Shiksha. (n.d.). Retrieved from Department of School Education & Literacy Ministry of Education, Government of India: https://samagra.education.gov.in/inclusive.html#:~:text=was%20being%20implemented.-,The%20Right%20to%20Free%20and%20Compulsory%20Education%20(RTE)%20Act%2C,and%20completion%20of%20elementary%20education.

Sharma, R. A. *Fundamentals of Special Education.* Meerut: R.Lall Book Depot.

Social Inclusion. (n.d.). Retrieved from The World Bank: https://www.worldbank.org/en/topic/social-inclusion#1

Umadevi, M. R. (2012). *Special Education.* Hyderabad: Neelkamal Publications Pvt. Ltd.